KU-223-552

BECOME A KEY PERSON OF INFLUENCE

5 Step Sequence to becoming one of the most highly valued and highly paid people in your industry.

Daniel Priestley

Become a Key Person of Influence
First published in 2010
Ecademy Press
48 St Vincent Drive
St. Albans, Hertfordshire, AL1 5SJ

This book is not intended to provide personalised legal, financial, or investment advice. The Authors and the Publisher specifically disclaim any liability, loss or risk which is incurred as a consequence, directly or indirectly, of the use and application of any contents of this work.

ISBN 978-1-905823-84-0

Illustrations: Andrew Priestley
Cover Design: Marcus Ubl & Andy Banjanin
Book Design: Marcus Ubl

Copyright © 2010 Daniel Priestley

The right of Daniel Priestley to be identified as the author of this work has been asserted in accordance with the Copyright Designs and Patents Act 1988.

All rights reserved. No part of this work may be reproduced in any material form (including photocopying or storing in any medium by electronic means and whether or not transiently or incidentally to some other use of this publication) without the written permission of the copyright holder except in accordance with the provisions of the copyright, Designs and Patents Act 1988. Applications for the copyright holders written permission to reproduce any part of this publication should be addressed to the publishers.

I dedicate this book to the people who use their power of influence to improve the world.

To those who promote better care and protection of the natural environment, reverence for animals, the rapid pursuit of human justice and the movement towards a humanity that is far more aware, I humbly dedicate this book to you.

I hope that the ideas in this book assist you in creating a world that works for everyone.

If ever you see a turtle sitting on a fence post, you can be sure he didn't get there on his own.

What others are saying about this book...

"Why be a 'worker-bee' when you could instead be a 'Key Person of Influence'? Daniel's book explains exactly how to get into the inner circle of any industry, fast. Read this book!"

- Mike Southon,
Financial Times columnist and best-selling business author.

"This book hits on the big trends of our time and shows you how leverage them to your advantage and to the advantage of the the people you meet. This is a must read."

- Thomas Power,
Founder of Ecademy.com and Co-Author of "A Friend In Every City".

"This book has very powerful ideas that will have you achieving much more in far less time. Hard work is not enough, if you want to make it big you must strive to become a Key Person of Influence. This book shows you exactly how to do that faster."

- Mike Harris,
Creator of 3 Multi-Billion Pound Businesses and Author of "Find Your Lightbulb".

CONTENTS

Introduction

At the center of every industry you will find an inner circle of people who are the most well known and valued people. They are the"Key People of Influence", or KPI's as they will be later known throughout this book.

You probably already know of these people in your industry:

Their names come up in conversation
...for all the right reasons.

They attract a lot of opportunities
... the right sort.

They earn a lot more money than most people
... and it isn't a struggle.

They can make a project successful if they are involved
... and people know it.

Key People of Influence enjoy a special status in their chosen field because they are well connected, well known, well regarded and highly valued. They get invited to be a part of the best teams and projects and they can often write their own terms.

Key People of Influence also have more fun. They get invited on trips away. People buy them dinner and drinks. They are treated with respect and others listen when they speak.

People think that it must take years or decades to become a Key Person of Influence (KPI). They think that KPIs need degrees or doctorates. They think KPIs must be gifted or from a wealthy family.

While time invested, qualifications, talents and a wealthy family are helpful, they are not a reliable way to make yourself a KPI.

There are plenty of people who have been in an industry for years who are NOT a Key Person of Influence. There are plenty of MBAs and PhDs who are NOT KPIs. There are people with talent and people born into privileged families who are not KPIs either.

And then there are the unusual stories like mine.

I arrived in the UK with nothing more than a suitcase and a credit card in 2006. I knew no one and I didn't have a lot of money.

Within three years, people started calling me one of the most connected entrepreneurs in London. I had built a business turning over millions and I could get on the phone to all of the high flyers and heavy hitters in my industry within a few calls.

All this in London; a city that is known for being a closed shop, full of 'Old Boy Networks'. I was told that it would be impossible to crack into the 'Establishment' and impossible to network 'above my station'.

How very wrong the critics were. London works like any other city in the world because it is full of people and people respond to the ideas I will talk about in this book wherever you go.

"It's not difficult to become a KPI in your industry in the next twelve months. But, you have to take the steps set out in this book and you have to do them very well"

If you do, you won't need to do more University training or spend decades climbing corporate ladders. You will become a Key Person of Influence in your field very fast.

This book contains powerful ideas

The chapters are set out in a particular order for a reason. There is a theme to this book and it's pretty obvious. I'm actually going to give you a five step sequence that will fast-track you towards KPI status.

Behind the obvious theme of this book and the five step KPI Formula, there is a hidden theme. There is a story behind the story you could say. It's more powerful than anything I say in this book overtly. It's not a secret but it's still hidden from most people.

When it becomes obvious to you, you will get a feeling and a sensation in your body. This hidden theme will click a lot of ideas into place quickly and it will trigger a rush of energy, insights and brainstorms. You might sit up through the night 'working' and still not be tired.

If you spot this hidden theme you will find it easy to earn lots of money and you will discover some very exciting trends. Your future will become crystal clear and you will know your next steps.

It's not a secret, but it is hidden from most people. It's worth taking the time to discover though. Maybe you will discover it the first time you read this book, maybe on the tenth time. Maybe it will hit you in the shower one morning and then you will re-read the book to confirm it.

Either way, don't give up on getting the real message; all the juice is in *'the story behind the story'*. It's in the chapters that you haven't examined that will point the way.

You might think that the chapters are out of order, that there are too many, or too few chapters. You might think that I haven't told you about the chapters you haven't seen yet. None of this is the case.

All the chapters are there for you to explore and when you can *'connect the dots'* you will step into the realm of the true KPI.

You will never fear not having money or influence again.

You will already have everything you ever need.

Part 1

The World Has Changed and So Must You

"We are living in a very different world today than we were just a decade ago. We're at the beginning of a whole new time.

We are no longer in the Industrial Age; we are in the Ideas Economy and everything has changed."

Looking Good Going Nowhere

I know an accountant. He is a great accountant however he's not happy and I know why. When he was 18 years old, fresh out of high school, his best thinking was to study for this job. He was good at maths and economics and for all the right reasons it made sense at the time to study and get into the accountancy profession.

Today he's frustrated. He's brilliant at what he does but he still has to compete on price. Like most of the people in his industry he thinks that the key to making more money is doing more study on the technical aspects of his job. Unfortunately for him, everyone in his business is focused at getting more qualifications and he finds himself constantly playing catch-ups. Regardless of how much he earns he still feels that he is only just slightly ahead of the game.

Lately he's been questioning everything; he feels that his life today is based upon the best thinking of an 18 year old. He has lived out 17 years of this teenager's decision and now he's in his mid 30s, his values have shifted and so has the world.

His story isn't unique. I hear it all the time. Many people are great at what they do but aren't fulfilled. Then the feeling creeps in that your life is passing year by year and the goals you had for yourself haven't been realised. You might even start questioning whether you made the right career choices.

By the end of this book you are going to see that you don't need to turn your life upside down. You don't need to go and do more study. You can forget the MBA and the PhD if you want. You can forget the get rich quick schemes that take you off track too.

If you follow what I am about to tell you in this book you will become a Key Person of Influence in your industry in the next six to twelve months. You'll enjoy yourself more, you'll make more money and it won't take you more time. You will even feel more sure of yourself.

However before I begin to share with you some of the actions that need to be done, we must first face up to some facts. We are living in a different world. It's not the same as it used to be. There are some new concepts you need to understand and some old ideas you need to let go of quickly.

If you are willing to do that, then let's begin.

Your Best Thinking Five Years Ago Is Your Baggage Today

In the last few years we have seen the explosive growth of social media, online shopping, massive breakthroughs in technology, a global recession and a massive shift towards entrepreneurship over employment.

In the last few years we have seen the economy change, the environment change, developing nations stride forward and the collective mind-set of the world has radically shifted too. All in just a few short years.

Your best thinking from five years ago is your baggage today.

Any decisions you made about your career, the location you lived, the technology you used, the people you associated with, the thought leaders you followed were all based upon a world that no longer exists.

Software I purchased five years ago for £10k+ is superseded by free web-based software today and what I dreamed of doing five years ago costs £50 a month!

Entrepreneurs I admired five years ago have lost their fortunes if they didn't shift their business model. Experts of five years ago are now scratching their heads.

Things people would pay for five years ago they expect for free today. Products that you used to shop retail for are freely available wholesale online.

The countries that offered the best opportunities for wealth creation five years ago are on their way to bankruptcy and are introducing socialist policies. The poor countries of just a few years ago are the powerhouses of tomorrow's free markets.

Unless we can let go of everything we currently think and do, we will fail to see the opportunities of tomorrow.

When Steve Jobs took over Apple in 1997 one of his first decisions was to get rid of the Apple Museum that occupied the foyer when people walked through the front door. He said that he refused to be in a company that was living in its past.

He didn't want the future of the company to be affected by the best thinking of its history. He wanted it to be living up to the best thinking of the future.

It's time to draw a line in the sand, take some time out and ask yourself the question:

> ***If I was starting completely fresh, in a world where anything is possible, what would I love to be doing?***

I haven't asked you what you should be doing. I've asked you what you would LOVE to be doing. If you are like most people, your passionate purpose is a lot closer than you think. There are parts of your business that you LOVE but you get pulled away to do the tasks you hate. Maybe you have a hobby you LOVE but the job you hate keeps you from it.

This book will reveal to you exactly how you can position yourself as a Key Person of Influence (KPI) in your field within the next twelve months. As a result you will attract opportunities, connections, ideas and resources that mean you will be able to do what you love and get paid what you are worth.

In this new exciting, changing world you will discover that it's the people who are doing what they LOVE who are thriving. If it feels like hard work, you will always get trumped by the person that has a passion for it.

So let's take a look at what lights you up.

Exercises ...

1. What comes easy to you that is harder for others?

2. If you had to do a month of 'work experience' in any industry, job, business or hobby, what would you do?

3. If you had to do something as a 'labour of love' what would you LOVE to do?

4. What did you discover about yourself when you answered these questions?

Notes ...

....

....

....

....

....

....

....

....

....

....

Vitality Is More Valuable Than Functionality

Key People of Influence are Vital People not Functional People. You can't get the results you want without a Vital Person. They are different to Functional People.

Functional People might be great at what they do, they might talk the talk and walk the walk but at the end of the day they are replaceable. If you can find a cheaper option you will take it because a functional person is just one solution to a problem. A Vital Person is the only solution.

Functional people see themselves as executing a set of processes. They try to get better at those processes and they make marginal improvements. Functional people worry about being downsized or overlooked. They are fearful that someone might come along who can 'do it' better.

Vital people see themselves as aligned to the result rather than the process.

No matter what, they will always be okay to adapt and change dynamically if it gets them towards a better result, or a faster result.

They feel like they own a specific piece of turf and no one could replace them. They see themselves as redefining the game in some way. They have their own unique take on things that makes them almost impossible to replace or overlook.

Functional people are scared to take a holiday. They worry what will happen while they are gone. Will they have a job to come back to? Will their clients find someone else? Will they lose opportunities they really need? A holiday is a scary thing to take when you are functional.

Vital people love taking holidays. They know that part of what makes them vital is that they have a certain spark that few people have and they have fresh ideas that people want to tap into. For a vital person a holiday is a place to get re-energised and to stimulate ideas. It's also a great reminder to everyone just how vital they are. A vital person knows that while they are gone, people are worried that they won't come back!

Functional people like to associate with people who reaffirm that life is tough. They like to be reassured that the economy is affecting others too and that times aren't what they used to be. A Functional Person loves the comfort of their friends who don't push them or inspire them to step up to a whole new level.

A Vital Person likes to be seen by their contemporaries.

They welcome challenging debate and stimulating ideas.

They want people to push them, to bring the best out of them and to stay true to the idea that there's always a new level to play at. A Vital Person will leave a group of people who slow them down for a group that stirs them up.

A Functional Person wants to get more
... A Vital Person wants to produce more.

A Functional Person wants to learn more
... A Vital Person wants to share more.

A Functional Person wants to be shown a path
... A Vital Person wants to create one.

A Functional Person is worn out by their functionality
... A Vital Person is re-energised by their vitality.

Want to see what a person of Vitality will do
(even after they have the money and the fame)
in order to keep pushing the boundaries?

Check out this video of David Blaine telling you
what he's willing to do in order to make "magic":

http://www.keypersonofinfluence.com/davidblaine

Exercises ...

1. Who do you know who is a Functional Person?

2. Who do you know who is a Vital Person?

3. What are some of the differences you notice between them?

Activity ...

Plan a holiday that would inspire you. Where have you been wanting to go but haven't yet? The Australian Outback? The Austrian Alps? The Brazilian Rainforest? The Canadian Rockies?

Now go to your diary and lock in a date. Call up the travel agent and buy a ticket. On holiday, you will get a sense of what's really important to you.

I'm serious.

Notes ...

....

....

....

....

....

....

Your Career Is Over

The concept of a career is like the fax machine. Sure enough, every office will probably have one lying around for a few more years yet, but it's only a matter of time before they figure out how to get rid of it. A career, like the fax machine was a good idea in the past but it simply has no big future. The world has moved on.

My grandfather had a career. He was accepted as an electrical apprentice in a factory, he worked hard and became a Technician, then a Foreman, a Junior Manager, a Manager and finally he retired as the General Manager of the company. He was with one company for 40 years. In this whole time he lived and worked in two cities.

My parents have had a few careers. Each spanning about ten years before they changed for something new. They have lived and worked in four cities each.

My sister has had several jobs and one business already. She's 21 years old. She's already lived and worked in three cities.

The US Department of Labour estimates that a worker who enters the labour force today will have 10-14 jobs by the time they are 38. In addition, never before has top talent been so mobile, living and working their way around the world.

It's easy to see where this trend is going. In the future we will see a massive trend towards 'Work on Demand'.

Just like in Hollywood teams come together to make a film project. They work on the project for six to twelve months and some of the people have multiple projects on the go at once. At the end of the project, everyone goes their separate ways. They might work together again on another project or they might not.

Employers aren't silly. They know that with increasingly strict labour laws, they can't run the risk of hiring people like they used to. They will outsource everything they can and only as a last resort will they hire people. If you are already in business, don't think that you are safe either. With the speed at which things are moving today, your business is going to have to reinvent itself constantly.

Almost every two years you're going to sit down and dream up a whole new plan for what you do and how you do it. If you don't, you'll be overtaken by those who do.

So if there's no security in jobs anymore and if small businesses are constantly changing, where does someone go to create certainty?

You go to your personal brand, your network, your experiences and your passion.

In the future your most valuable asset is the number of people who know you, like you and trust you. In the future, you will be defined by 'your take on things'.

In the future, you will discover that what you do has changed but your passion has only become stronger.

From now on, you personally must see yourself as being in an enterprise that others get to know about. If you are in a job, your 'enterprise' sells a result that your employer wants. Currently your method of delivery is showing up for eight to ten hours a day. If you are in business, you and your business need to become known for something unique.

You won't be known for the place that you work; you will be known for the people you're connected to and the ideas you are immersed in. Once these things are known, you will have a constant stream of opportunities coming your way.

Your career may be dead but as a Key Person of Influence your adventure is just beginning.

The Harder You Work The Less You Earn

> ***"Your best ideas will come out to play ... not to work"***

In the modern economy, hard work is not a competitive advantage anymore; everyone works hard.

If you were to gather up all the hardest working people in the world you would not find the top CEOs and the

Entrepreneurs, you would find the people who are struggling to make it up the ladder or struggling to survive at all.

The competitive advantage is in thinking expansively, connecting with the right people and spotting fresh opportunities.

With that in mind, a week of sailing with friends in Spain could yield you more ideas, connections and perspective than a week of answering emails, catching up on paperwork and attending meetings.

As I said, I believe that the difference between the successful people on the planet is not Functionality, it's Vitality. Functionality is about performing a task well, whereas Vitality is about doing it joyfully.

In the last ten years we have seen machines and systems replace a whole lot of Functionality in the workplace however we are a long, long way from seeing the first machine that can compete with raw human Vitality.

If you look at the top earners, they don't consider what they do to be work. They are playing a game that they love and they make sure that it stays fun. They exude a level of vitality for what they do and because they love it, they get good at it too.

The minute you begin to feel yourself 'working hard' as opposed to 'playing a challenging game' it's time to take a break.

Disappear for a week, get some sun, read up on your favourite role models, explore fresh ideas and spend time with people who are 'in their zone'.

More than anything, reconnect with your humanity. Beneath your desire to have a great home, a snappy wardrobe and some money in the bank is a part of you that longs to make a difference as well. Getting in touch with this part of you will give you a broadband connection to your Vitality.

From a place of Vitality all the work comes easily, the ideas flow freely and the money comes in more effortlessly. A week of play will do more for your career or business than a week of work. An hour of inspiration is worth more than a week of drudging on.

Success isn't about engaging in a struggle; it is about getting into flow.

Exercises ...

Here's a couple of great questions you might want to explore:

- What would I LOVE to do this week?
- Who would I LOVE to spend some time with (reading a great biography could count)?
- Where would I LOVE to be going this week?
- How would I LOVE to deliver more value to others?
- What difference would I LOVE to make on the planet?

If you get stuck with the answers to these questions, you know what to do ...

As scary as it might seem, pick up the phone and book yourself a week away.

Notes ...

....

....

....

....

....

....

The Eiffel Tower and The Parisian Landscape

There was a time when Paris became unpopular and its citizens started moving abroad.

Although Paris had a beautiful landscape, there was no focal point in the city, nothing exciting or iconic to really put it on the map and the people got bored.

Then one day Mr Eiffel put up his tower and the culture rapidly changed. People who had visited Paris showed their photos and soon people all over the world came in droves to see the Eiffel Tower. It was interesting, unique, distinct and had a certain je ne sais quoi.

Once people were in Paris they discovered the beautiful landscape and decided to stick around. They spent money in the shops, galleries and hotels and the city became vibrant again.

Big businesses understand this. On Facebook, users being able to 'tag' friends was the 'Eiffel Tower' idea. Apple customers proudly display their iPods with the iconic white headphones. Nike pays the best athletes in the world to be their 'Eiffel Tower'.

You will need to create something exciting about yourself that people want to tell others about. It's going to have to be unique to you. Something that puts you on the map. Later in this book you will see that getting clear on your micro-niche will draw people to you.

You will also see that being an author of the right kind of book is one of the best ways you can create an 'Eiffel Tower' for yourself.

You also need a landscape - a place where people can become a 'citizen' of your brand.

Once someone finds you, they need a suite of products and experiences that they can take part in. Apple customers eventually buy the computers as well as the iPods and then they can't switch back to a PC. Aspiring tennis players see Rafael Nadal wearing Nike and then buy the clothes and the shoes and the rackets and they are 'Niked'.

You will need some products that people can adopt as their own. For example, they might hear that you have a very unique take on things and that you're an author of a book, they might read it and like the ideas. Then they will want to get the audio workshop or the DVD. They will want to join your online group, read your regular blog updates and follow your twitter feed. C'est tres bien! They are now a citizen of your brand.

Already, you should be beginning to ask yourself...

1. *What is my flagship idea that people get talking about? What core ideas am I known for? What is unique about my story? What can people agree is an icon for me or my business? What do people want to come and see/hear/sense from me? What do people keep asking me about at a dinner party?*

2. *When people come and see me and then like what I do, what can I do to make them feel like a 'citizen' of my brand? How can my ideas and products become part of their everyday life? How can I get them to feel more connected with me long term?*

With an 'Eiffel Tower' and a beautiful 'landscape' you are on your way to being a Key Person of Influence.

Don't worry if you haven't got all the answers just yet; later in this book I'm going to share the five things you can do that will rapidly achieve these goals.

For now though, I want to share with you why NOW is the most exciting time in history to get these things right and to establish yourself as a KPI.

The Internet Has Changed Everything

The internet has changed the business landscape massively in the last five years and in 2010 and beyond new opportunities and challenges are emerging.

Google allows people to find very specific information. New Media allows people to connect with like-minded individuals around the world. E-commerce allows you to sell products to a global marketplace.

In the next ten years we will see the effects and they will be huge. So far the internet has been in development, but only now are people starting to connect the dots with all of this new, free (or cheap) technology.

> ***Remember that there is always a lag time between the release of new technology, its uptake and the impact it has***

One thing we know for sure, whenever there is a new and more powerful way to connect and communicate, it has a huge impact on business. Phones, commercial air travel, television, email and mobile computing have all shown us that the companies that adapt quickly get a jump on those that don't.

It's now possible for a 17 year old girl sitting in her bedroom to start a group on Facebook for free. She can have thousands of followers and fans worldwide ... for free.

She can talk to them all on video... for free! She can write to them all ... for free. She can get them all excited about her ideas...... FOR FREE! You get the idea?

This teenager can create or source a product easily and cheaply. She can design a brand easily and cheaply. She can have a web-store easily and cheaply. She can take payment easily and cheaply. She can send her products whizzing around the world easily and cheaply. And all from her bedroom.

These are the times we live in. Already we are seeing people as young as 20 making six figure incomes from their crazy ideas.

Most people think that these 'whiz kids' are succeeding because they are good with technology but this is not the reason.

These teenagers aren't stuck to the idea that a business has to be the way it used to be. They don't think a brand needs to cost a lot of money or that they need to live in a particular geography. They don't think that the idea needs to please everyone or that they need to meet their clients face to face in order to deliver a powerful experience.

That's why they are succeeding; not because they are better at using the technology. They are better at letting go of the past ideas, probably because they were never attached to them in the first place.

The game has changed

The game has fundamentally changed. The internet, social media and the mobile-web will change everything.

Just like 150 years ago when the game changed. The Industrial Revolution introduced new technology that changed everything.

The people who used machines made fortunes and the people who stuck to their old ways ended up on the factory floor.

The economy is always looking for a better product for a lower price. For the last 150 years big companies who could afford big factories were the only ones able to deliver it. But not any more, not in the Ideas Economy.

Small business can deliver better quality at a lower cost. Small businesses can source products and ideas faster and cheaper over the internet than big businesses can. Small enterprise can access big factories when they need to but don't have the overheads when they aren't using them.

Small is faster. Small is more dynamic. Small is cheaper. Small is more flexible. Small is more fun. And small can look big.

Best of all, Small has the feeling that it was made bespoke for you. Rather than buying things that everyone has, you can have unique things that were made for people 'just like you'.

If you are a Vegetarian and you want to go to the gym, you can learn from the world's best Vegetarian Bodybuilder. He could give you recipes, workout routines and products made just for vegetarian bodybuilders.

If you love vintage Mercedes-Benz convertibles from the 1960's but you hate the ones made from the 1970's onwards, there is a group you can join. There are blogs for people like you and videos and downloads and web stores to buy from. There will be a 'hero' you admire because she hates the 1970's cars just as much as you do and she has a mint condition 1963 SL280.

If you love reading about Deep Sea Free-Diving you can read the blogs from world champions. You can watch their home movies, listen to interviews with them, keep track of their adventures and even buy the same gear that they use.

On the internet, you are not some freak who is too fussy or who has strange taste. You are part of a 'tribe', a gang of people who believe as you believe. This gang has conversations that 'regular people' wouldn't understand.

This gang has leaders. This gang has thousands and thousands and thousands of members.

This is a fundamental shift that big business just can't cater to. IKEA can't make 'one of a kind' furniture. Microsoft can't make special software especially for owners of tattoo parlours. Flight Center can't advertise travel packages just for Jewish singles who love rock climbing.

It's all too hard for big business but it's all too easy for small entrepreneurs on the internet. Never has there been a better time to be a small entrepreneur.

Key Ideas ...

- People can search the internet for everything and anything.
- In the future they will want things that were made 'just for people like them'.
- Big business can't cater for these specific requirements and small highly niched businesses will emerge as very profitable and fun places to be 'working'.

Activity ...

Go online and search for your specific interests. Don't just search Google. Have a look on Facebook, Twitter, YouTube and Ning. Get really specific and see what comes up.

Notes ...

....

....

....

....

....

....

....

....

The story of the happy lawyer with the ripped up jeans.

Recently I attended a breakfast event and was seated next to a commercial lawyer. Naturally we kicked off the conversation with the age old question, "What do you do?"

I was interested to discover that he had been a lawyer for a big corporate consulting firm but had recently set up his own home-based, private practice.

At his previous job he had just five hedge fund clients to service. Each day he would get up at 6:30am put on the suit and tie, fight the commute into town, sit in a stale corporate environment and then fight his way home in time for dinner at 7pm.

He was well aware that his charge-out rate was several times what he was being paid. So one very brave day, he decided to hand in his notice and, along with two others like him, set up in private practice (based out of their individual home offices).

No sooner had this happened, his five hedge fund clients followed him loyally into his new venture and continued taking his counsel. The only difference is that they pay about 65% of the fees they were paying before (most of the money they were spending went into the city offices, the golf sponsorships, the middle managers, the senior managers, the magazine ads, the gifts, the bonuses, etc).

So now, the clients pay less and get a better service, he has an extra two hours a day that aren't spent commuting and he's earning more money than ever before.

Better still, he told me that sometimes he does video conversations with his clients from home with a jacket, shirt and tie up top and a pair of ripped jeans under the desk.

I personally don't think this is an isolated example, to me this is the shape of things to come in an economy where big business has a hard time competing with KPIs in their own small business.

At one of my events I told this story,
you can watch the quick video here:
www.keypersonofinfluence.com/rippedjeans

If you like, feel free to share it with someone you know who is sick of being a corporate slave.

Now is the time to be a Key Person of Influence

I could not have written this book 150 years ago. Back then there were only two types of people - those who could afford a factory and those who could not. There would be no point in telling people to go for their dreams; they simply didn't have any means of production to be Vital, they had to be Functional or they would starve.

Even fifteen years ago I couldn't have written this book. You still needed to be a generalist. No one could find you if you had a business that did something specialised and arty. Big companies still controlled all of the niches and you had to work within their structure.

Today all that has changed. Today the 'factory' costs almost nothing (a laptop, a phone, a website and a passion). And since the whole world can find you once you start taking your ideas online, every industry has broken down into sub-categories of little niches within niches. I call these 'micro-niches'.

Every industry you can imagine can be broken down into niches and micro-niches and each one needs a KPI.

When someone asks, *"Who's the best wedding make-up artist in Majorca?"* you will be able to google them and find them easily.

In every niche and micro-niche there will be Key People of Influence. There is virtually a limitless demand for KPIs in the world right now.

In the next ten years there will be huge advantages for people who stand out as a Key Person of Influence in their chosen field.

Teams will form around them, people will track them down from around the world and the top money will flow to those who step up to be a KPI in their industry.

Fortunately you are at the beginning of a trend. Things are possible today that were not possible just a few years ago. You are a 'first settler' in a 'brave new world'.

The Brave New World

I am an Australian and I was brought up hearing the stories about the 'First Settlers' in that 'Brave New World' in the 1800s.

In that time it was an agricultural economy so in order to create wealth and power these first settlers staked their claim to a piece of land. This became the place they built their wealth and it was the place they could be found.

People who failed to claim a piece of land wandered around aimlessly doing odd jobs for the people who owned the land. These itinerant workers were called Swagmen because they carried their rolled-up sleeping bags called swags on their backs on bush tracks. They had no place to call home and they just kept wandering around looking for work.

After a while all the land was taken and they were stuck feeling resentful that they hadn't claimed their land when they had the chance. They complained that they worked hard and didn't get paid enough.

In the Ideas Economy the first settlers create wealth and power by staking their claim to niche (or a micro niche - a niche within a niche). This is the place that people can find you. Others quickly figure out where you stand and they can send the right people your way.

Owning a Micro-Niche is as valuable as owning land. If you are known as a Key Person of Influence in your field you will attract the money and the opportunities that are flowing around you. Even if you pass those opportunities to others, your wealth and power grows.

Some people in the ideas economy aren't staking their claim to a niche. They are the modern day 'swagmen' who just wander around looking at the other people who have claimed their 'land'. They want to try and please everyone but they don't attract anyone. They keep coming up with new ideas but aren't brave enough to settle on something and really give it a go.

After a while all the Micro-Niches in their industry will have thriving KPIs and these wandering Swagmen will wish they had claimed their place sooner. They will resent the KPIs and say *"I could have done that"*, but they didn't, instead they became an aimless wanderer who will end up working for a KPI. Do you want to be a swaggie or a KPI?

Now is the time to claim your micro-niche. It's the time to say,

> ***I won't try to be all things to all people. This is exactly what I do and this is my unique take on things***

Some examples of Niches and some Micro-Niches:

Niche: Heath and Wellness
Micro-Niches: Raw Food Parties, Fresh Juice Delivery, 10 Day De-toxing Retreat, Spirulina Supplements in Cakes, Vegetarian Marathons.

Niche: Small Business Services
Micro-Niches: Hair Salon Marketing Advice, Facebook Advertising Agency, Testimonial Video Production in Manchester, Alerts on Distressed Advertising Space.

Niche: House and Family
Micro-Niches: News and Advice for Divorced Fathers, Dog furniture for Cocker Spaniels, Accelerated Learning for Toddlers, Painting Portraits of Owners with their Horses.

Niche: Clothing and Apparel
Micro-Niches: Socks with motivational quotes on them, Clothing that works with iPods, Non-leather 'leather' jackets, fashion advice for CEOs of publicly traded companies in New York.

Niche: Travel
Micro-Niche: Jewish Singles Travel, Cruises for over 65s, Follow the F1 Circuit for a year, Diving to Rebuild a Reef.

In every industry there are going to be Micro-Niches within the Niches.

Each Micro-Niche will be an opportunity for a KPI to claim it as their 'land'.

The internet will allow people from all over the world to find that KPI and do business with them.

People who fail to claim a Micro-Niche will wish they had.

Exercises ...

- What industry do you enjoy spending your time in?
- Make a list of Micro-Niches in that industry (Think: Gender, Geography, Specialty, Common Interest).
- Google some of these Micro-Niches to see if someone has already claimed this land.

Activity ...

Create a mock-up brochure for yourself as the KPI in a micro-niche. See how it feels to claim this space as your own.

Notes ...

....

....

....

....

....

....

....

....

....

....

You already have a unique set of skills and talents

The very good news is that in this'new found land', almost anything can be turned into a fun, profitable business with a little bit of thought.

Your greatest asset is your existing passion, the skills you already have and most of all your own personal story.

You may think that the key to your wealth lies in some fan-dangle wealth creation vehicle that you don't yet know about. Maybe you think it's the Stock Market or the Property Game, or a Franchise or Multi-Level-Marketing company.

The truth is that your real wealth lies in your story. Your journey thus far has not been a waste of time; it's been perfect. Your hobbies and interests are not meaningless, they are a gold mine. Your passion isn't hollow; it's the best fuel you will ever have.

Quite literally there are already people taking home six figure incomes from their passion for the strangest things.

I've seen people make great money:

- Teaching people to do their make-up to look like comic book characters.
- Selling mobile phone covers that are covered in fake diamonds.

- Teaching beginners how to play U2 songs on guitar.
- Giving business advice on setting up in Asia.
- Running an annual amateur yacht race in Thailand.
- Selling little bags of organic mixed nuts that help give you a colon cleanse.

But here's the problem. Everyday you will open the paper and read about some guy or girl who has made big money doing some new thing. You hear a story about some newly made millionaire who's achieving success in some strange and different industry.

The assumption you may wrongly make is that it was the 'thing' that made the money. You might think it was the product or the industry that was responsible for their success and not the marriage of that 'thing' with that person.

"Oh, if only I was in the property game".

"Of course, it's FOREX Trading I should be doing".

"Why didn't I think of being an NLP Master sooner".

"What was I thinking not being a Dog Cleaning Franchisee last year".

"Silly me, I knew I should have been part of that exotic juice MLM from the start".

THEIR thing might not be YOUR thing.

What you may miss altogether is the story behind the story ...

The person who just made it from real estate loved real estate for a long time before they got rich.

The person who trades the markets was happy riding through the ups and downs for a long time before they just seemed to 'get it right'.

The NLP Life Coach did three years of unpaid work in the industry before they got their break.

And so on and so forth.

It's their story that people buy into. You like them. You like their take on things. You like their ideas. You see how connected they are in their industry.

You want to spend time and money with them because they are a KPI and that's attractive to you.

The person in the story hasn't found THE thing, they have found THEIR thing. However, I could almost guarantee that it's not YOUR thing.

Unless you have been keenly interested in something for at least seven years, forget trying to be a success story in that field.

You simply can't out-do the people who genuinely love that industry, not because they think it is a quick formula for cashing in.

But wait a minute. Aren't I contradicting myself? Didn't I say earlier in this book that it takes just twelve months to become a Key Person of Influence? Now I'm saying seven years! No, I said ...

"How to become one of the most connected, visible, accessible and valuable people in your industry ... in the next twelve months"

The most important word in that sentence is 'your'. You already have a story, you already have a set of skills, talents and experiences that are valuable.

There is already a theme to your life that has been unfolding. It may seem that you have done many things or that you have some strange and unrelated talents, but it hasn't been random at all. Everything you have done up until this point has been for a specific reason. It has brought you right here, to this chapter in this book where you can get this message.

> ***You are already standing on a mountain of value. Your story is valuable, your experience is unique, you are worth your weight in gold ... just as you are!***

You don't need to learn new skills; you are ready to create value. You are no longer on this planet to be a consumer; you are here to be a producer.

"All of your future learnings will come from the process of producing value."

This may rattle you a little. Surely, if you were valuable already you would already have the money? No, the reason you don't have the money is because you have not yet established yourself as a KPI and you haven't crystalised your value into products. In the next few chapters you will see exactly how to do this in five clear steps.

When you are ready, let's take a look.

Exercises ...

- Map out the timeline of your life with high points and low points. Start out as early as you can remember and try to remember some of the details for each memory.
- Once you have your life's timeline, look for the themes - were you with groups? Were you outdoors? Were you the leader?
- Make a list of you skills and talents on separate pieces of paper and see if you can join them up. Eg: Bilingual-Archery-Consultant.

Activity ...

On your bathroom mirror stick a sign that reads:

"I am already standing on a mountain of value. My story is valuable, my experience is unique, I am worth my weight in gold just as I am.

All of my future learnings will come from the process of me producing value."

Notes ...

....

....

....

....

....

....

Part 2

The Five Step Sequence to Becoming a Key Person of Influence

"In business a KPI is a Key Performance Indicator. It is a benchmark that people measure themselves against. Likewise, a Key Person of Influence sets a standard that others aspire to. If you become a Key Person of Influence people will associate you with the level of performance they want to emulate".

How do you become a Key Person of Influence ... faster?

In every industry there's an inner circle of KPIs. If there's a good opportunity going in their industry, these people are the first to be told. If they don't like the opportunity they pass it to another KPI. If all the KPIs don't like the opportunity they kick it out to the outer circle.

This sets up an interesting situation. The inner circle is rich with good opportunities shared between a small number of people. The outer circle is full of many people fighting over the poor opportunities.

For this reason, until you are in that inner circle of KPIs, your full time job is to become a KPI.

Let me illustrate my point.

I have been a public speaker and an event producer for over eight years now. I run big events with world class speakers covering topics like Leadership, Growth, Branding, Trends and Entrepreneurship.

In my time running business events and speaking at events around the world I have seen well over 100,000 business people in the audiences.

Before the event begins, I often watch people networking and what I see has given me some unique insights.

Most people are abysmal at generating any attraction with others. Most people walk away from a business event with nothing more than a small stack of business cards from people who have no interest in doing any business with them.

It's not because they are bad people, or that they don't have any value to share. It's simply that they have never been taught how to represent themselves as a KPI.

I also experience this first hand when people approach me directly.

At almost every event I've ever run, someone will come up to me and say ...

I would love to be a professional speaker. How do I get myself up on the stage?

They often add to that question: *"I've done some speaker training and I am a confident speaker"*.

At this point, I don't care if they are the best speaker in the world. First, I need to know if they are a Key Person of Influence. So I ask some questions ...

1. What's your specialty or niche?

I want to know that they genuinely stand out for one thing, but unfortunately most of them give me an answer that actually puts me off.

They say something like, *"I motivate people to be their best"* or something as vague as, *"I help people get what they want"* or something as general as, *"I help businesses grow."*

2. What makes you think people would pay to turn up and see you speak. What makes you credible?

I ask *"Do you have a book? Do you have a big online following? Has your story attracted a lot of media attention?"*

Most people fumble and feel awkward that they have no proof of their value. They say *"I've been doing this for 14 years"* or *"I have some good testimonials"*.

3. What products do you offer?

"Do you have a CD set? Do you have a Workshop on DVD? Do you have a product that I can experience and get a sense of what you are all about?"

Most of the time their "product" is them. They need to physically turn up in order for the client to get value.

Conversely, they may have a product but it's so generic that I instantly compare it to other products in the market.

Finally I ask, *"What will happen when someone googles you"?*

- Will impressive videos of you come up on YouTube?
- Will I be able to download some of your audio feeds?
- Will I see that you have thousands of Twitter followers?
- Or, will some guy in Florida with the same name come up? Some random guy who has nothing to do with you or your business? At that point of my search I would lose interest.

What many of these aspiring public speakers fail to realise is that speaking opportunities do not go to well-trained speakers. They go to Key People of Influence.

When a KPI approaches me, doing a deal is easy; but their approach is radically different. A KPI knows their micro-niche, a KPI will hand me a copy of their book, a KPI will tell me about the proven track record of their products and a KPI will be all over the internet (for all the right reasons) when you google them. After that, it's a no-brainer to track them down and figure out a good deal to do.

This isn't only true for the public speaking industry. Across all industries, the top opportunities go directly to a small group of people who present themselves as a Key Person of Influence in that field. The rest of the people in the industry are left to fight over the opportunities that the KPI's turned down.

It's not that hard to become a KPI and it certainly doesn't take years to achieve. There's just five things that you need to have in place for you to demonstrate that you are a KPI:

1. Pitch | Know & communicate your micro-niche.
Key People of Influence can answer the question *"what do you do?"* with power and clarity.

It's not enough to have a niche. You need a niche within a niche (a micro-niche) and you need to be able to communicate it. A niche is Bodybuilding, a micro-niche is Vegetarian Bodybuilding, or 12 Week Transformations, or Christian Bodybuilding in New York.

When you know exactly the specific game that you're playing, you don't just make more money, you also have more fun, attract greater opportunities and experience more rewards.

2. Publish | Gain credibility through a book.
Your book is the "Title Deed" to your Micro-Niche, it tells the world that you are an authority in your field. It's no coincidence that the word "Authority" has the word "Author" in it.

It isn't hard to write a book if you plan it and execute it correctly. It will take you twelve months (tops) from the day you sit and jot down your concept to the day you open up a box full of books with your face on them.

These days you can publish very short runs of books (you

could start by ordering 20 copies of your book) and it's easy to make it available globally on Amazon.com.

Add a few shining reviews (from people who know and like you) and all of a sudden you're a published author(ity), praised by your readers with a global online distribution.

3. Productise | Turn what you know into product.

Turning your skill-set into an asset is an essential part of becoming a KPI. An information product (such as a CD, DVD, Download, etc) opens up a world of opportunities. Behind every talented person or dynamic business are great ideas and those ideas need to be shared.

An information product can also be a high value, high margin product that can add considerable profit to your enterprise.

It's not difficult to create a digital information product. Some careful planning, a day with a voice or video recorder (and no kids in the background), a small amount spent with an AV guy and you'll have a product ready to manufacture.

Now you can provide value to people all over the world. A good CD or DVD kit can sell for £29 - £5,000+ depending on the content.

4. Profile | Raise your profile and Google well.

These days, if Google thinks you are a nobody ... you are a nobody. When people do a search for your name, it must come up on the first results page that you are a Key Person of Influence in your chosen field. Provided your name isn't Brad Pitt this isn't as challenging as you think.

Invest a few days of focused effort and you can have a dozen social-networking profiles, a Twitter account with 400-plus followers, several YouTube videos and a dozen blogs.

With all that in place you are going to sky-rocket up the Google listings. Staying there will require you to be diligent, but if you are organised, that can take less than 20 minutes a day (and it could be done from your iPhone in the back of a cab).

When you have those four things in place, NOW you're ready to approach people about this final fifth step ...

5. Partnering | Forge Joint Ventures & Partnerships.

Like you might have guessed, the real wealth comes when you complete this final stage and begin leveraging with others in an effective way.

Consider that there is already someone who has a list of 10,000 potential customers for your product. There are already experts in your industry who would jump at the chance to be interviewed by you to create a product that enhances their brand (and yours).

There are already people who have products that your contacts would be interested in and they would happily pay you a percentage.

The hopefuls who want to be speakers at my events clearly understand the power of a Joint Venture Partnership.

They know I could put them in front of a large audience and from that platform, they would generate countless opportunities. However they are trying to leap straight to Step Number 5 without doing the first four things.

The real money is made from JVs and partnerships but JVs and partnerships don't happen until people know that you are a KPI. The fastest way to become a KPI in your industry is by doing the first four things (Pitch, Publish, Productise and Profile).

When you have these steps in place, you will be amazed at what happens to your life. You will be asked to speak at events, you will be referred to as an 'expert', you will get more focused opportunities coming your way, you will be able to access most people in your industry and you will earn more money with less struggle.

You will become a person of vitality rather than a person of functionality.

These five keys are the cornerstones of becoming a KPI. It's not about late-nights swatting over text books, getting more qualifications, or putting in another few years hard slog in the office. The faster you can get these five steps completed well, the faster you will be a KPI.

So when you're ready, turn the page and let's explore these five stages of becoming a KPI in more detail.

KPI STEP 1:
Your Perfect Pitch

Your 'perfect pitch' is so much more than you think. The truth is, with a perfect pitch you will be swamped with opportunities.

Consider that many of the greatest wealth creators and change-makers throughout history started with little more than a persuasive pitch. Armed with nothing more than their eloquent words they set about changing the world.

Here are some excerpts from Perfect Pitches that changed the world:

"I have a dream that some day this nation will live up to its creed that all men are created equal" - **Dr King Jr**

"We choose to go to the moon by the end of this decade, not because it's easy but because it's hard" - **JFK**

"We will put a computer in every home and in every office across America" - **Bill Gates**

"You must be the change you want to see in the world."
- **Mahatma Gandhi**

"Imagine all the people, living for today" - **John Lennon**

Can you imagine asking these visionaries, *"What do you do for a living?"*

Their response would be so exhilarating, provocative and contagious that you would want to help them in any way you could. That is how you want people to react to your ideas too.

I often ask business people to rate themselves on how well they think they answer the question "What do you do?"

Most give themselves 7 or 8 out of 10, but is this realistic?

Consider that everyone you meet knows over 250 people. A 10 out of 10 would mean they want to tell everyone about you. They would want to phone their most prized contacts and introduce you. A 10 out of 10 means that people will openly share their time, contacts and resources with you.

With this in mind, most people rate 1 to 2 out of 10 at best. They leave over 80 per cent of potential on the table in every single interaction.

Don't be discouraged, get excited. There is massive room to grow just by improving the way you describe what you are up to in the world.

When someone asks you the quintessential networking question *"What do you do?"* your enthralling answer will have the power to unlock all of their resources.

A not-so-potent answer will elicit a polite response but nothing much will come of the interaction.

Beware of the Polite Response

A polite comment is one of the worst responses you can get when you tell people what you do. It is polite responses that keep you 'looking good but going nowhere'. You can go nowhere for years because of polite responses.

Most people think it is encouraging that others nod and smile. When someone says *"Sounds interesting"* or *"How long have you been doing that?"* it is actually a meaningless non-response. They are being polite, but in truth are not engaged or interested.

What you want is an emotionally-charged response. They should either love it or they hate it. Ideally, you want to see some immediate action.

You want people to engage with you. They should either pull out their diary and make a time to talk to you, put you in touch with someone they know or they should tell you emphatically: *"Your idea will never work!"*

This strong reaction is much better than a polite, benign response because you know that they are really listening and considering your ideas, not dismissing you. You will have stirred up a reaction and made a connection.

Speaking With Power

It isn't just one-to-one interactions that you Perfect Pitch comes out to play. The day you get invited to speak in front of a group or to the media is the day your life can change dramatically.

I have seen great speakers take the stage, share their vision and rally incredible amounts of support. I have seen a 45 minute talk raise millions, I have seen an 8 minute pitch that resulted in over 250 people rushing to grab a business card from the presenter (it held up the event by over 30 minutes).

I've watched 18 minute talks that have changed my life forever (on TED.com).

When you know "what you are up to in the world" you become a magnet for opportunity. When you can communicate that message to a group, you speed up time and can achieve a months work in a day. People see your vision, they see you leading the way and they come rushing at you with every resource you could every need, want or imagine.

But who are you to command that attention? Who are you, to have people rushing your way? What's so special about you? Let's find out.

You Are Already Standing On A Mountain Of Value

Remember, your story is already more valuable than you think. Don't dare throw out your history. Sometimes it is simply a case that it is difficult to see your own value and you need to speak with others about your ideas and dreams.

Where I grew up in Queensland, Australia there is an ancient ridge of volcanic mountains called the Glass House Mountains. We would climb the imposing giant Mount Tibrogargan.

From the summit you get a view of how massive all the other smaller mountains are and it doesn't feel like you are standing on the tallest mountain of the group. From that lofty vantage point, the peaks are equalised.

Most people are already standing on a mountain of value however it is difficult to see the size and shape and attributes of the mountain when you are on it. When you look down all you see is the dirt beneath your feet and when you look up you see how impressive the other mountains are.

It is very easy to see value from a distance, so you see the value in others so effortlessly but you sometimes fail to notice the immense value in yourself.

This is why you need to engage with some trusted friends and even some objective people you don't know to get their input. You need to get someone else to reflect back to you what they see as your value and how it should be packaged.

In a perfect world you would sit down with a multi-millionaire entrepreneur, a marketing expert or a professional coach with an impeccable track record.

This dynamic team would take you through a process of

questioning and make suggestions until you had a 'Perfect Pitch'.

People who have worked with our team, discover that their story is already of amazing value when pitched correctly. One of the most exhilarating things I get to witness on a regular basis is when someone breaks through and sees how much they have to offer the world, just as they are.

Sometimes it is overwhelming to people when they see what they have been hiding. It's like discovering you have an original Van Gogh sitting in your basement! Many people unlock a burst of energy they never knew they had.

At the least, you must ask some friends and clients to help you with this discovery. It will be one of the greatest things you do.

Discover Your 'Big Game'

One of my mentors is a man who has built three multi-billion pound businesses. He has personally secured hundreds of millions worth of investment for his ideas. He knows how to create a powerful pitch.

He says that at the heart of a 'Perfect Pitch' is a Mission, which he calls 'Your Big Game' that you and your business want to be known for.

Your perfect pitch is your "why". It's your compass. It's the reason you get up each day.

Bill Gates said Microsoft's big game was *"To put a Personal Computer in every home and on every desk in the world"*.

Ray Kroc said that McDonald's big game was *"If Man Goes To The moon we will go there too, open a restaurant and serve him a great burger at a great price."*

Oprah Winfrey said her big game was to *"Share a daily dose of inspiration with women all over the world"*.

My big game is to *"Lead people out of the Industrialised Workforce and into the Entrepreneur Revolution so they can earn great money doing what they love and be free to make a difference as well"*.

Your Big Game should:

- Get you out of bed rearing to go in the morning and keep you up late at night.
- Become the heart of how you design your business and how you get results.
- Become the source of the irresistibly delightful experience you deliver to everyone who comes into contact with you.

Your perfect pitch is not just a set of well-rehearsed words. It is a statement about what you are up to in the world. It's your big game that lights you up just thinking about it.

Here's some of the components of a good game:

It must be fun: There is no point playing a game that is no fun. Sure enough it will have its share of struggles, it will have its frustrations and at times it may seem impossible. But underneath the challenges, it will still be an exciting and fun game you want to get up each day and play.

It must have rules: There are clear structures, time frames and behaviour that is 'out-of-bounds'. You must be able to explain to people 'the rules of the game'. Someone on your team might ask, *"Why do we spend so much time with customers after they already buy from us?"* to which you might say, *"One of the rules for the game is that we must have customers who feel respected and appreciated by us and rate us at least 8/10 on customer service".*

There must be players: Every game has players who come to the game because they consider their strengths are well suited to the game. The better your players the more fun the game. It's fun to watch the NBA because all the players are almost super human. Your game should be set up in a way that top players want to join you to demonstrate their abilities.

There must be a prize: Committed players love to play for the fun of the game but when you have a coveted prize at stake everything goes to the next level. Is it money? Is it ownership? Is it recognition? Is it something even bigger? What ever it is, the prize must be exciting for the players.

There must be a way to win: Imagine a game that has no end time. Imagine a game that doesn't keep score. Imagine a game where there is no clear way to win. It would not be fun and it would not keep people interested.

As the game master, you will need to make sure you know when you are winning and just how you will know when you have won. Just like professional sporting events, your game should offer short-term wins as well as an overall championship victory. The thought of winning should stir you up emotionally and make you feel a surge of energy and focus.

There must be a way to lose: If you can't lose the game then it's no fun either. The game must be edgy enough that the players realise it's entirely possible to lose.

The thought of losing the game should be a strong driver and there should be a point where it is clear the game has been lost so players know when it's time to go back to the locker room and rethink their strategy.

The question you must ponder again and again is this...

> ***What's the 'big game' you would love to play over the next three to five years ... Win or Lose?***

The answer needs to make you feel enlivened. When you have that answer you are ready to construct your Perfect Pitch around your Big Game.

Exercises ...

- Write the words 'My Big Game' in the centre of a piece of paper and mind map the important factors for you.
- Make sure you have at least three to five insights for each of the six elements in your Big Game.

Notes ...

You Can't Please Everyone

The next point to be sure of is that you have a specific Micro-Niche; a place that you can start your big game from.

Even a massive phenomenon like Facebook started out exclusively for Harvard University students to share their drunken photos, they then expanded to allow all university students. From a tiny Micro-Niche big things can grow but it almost never happens that a business sets out to please everyone and actually achieves it.

You need to consider your industry niche carefully and then add more criteria. You need to know exactly who you are you showing up for.

Is your business going to specialise in a gender, an age group, a geography, a socio-economic group?

Will you focus on a specific need, common beliefs and values or a common frustration or problem of a specific group?

More often than not, YOU will be the micro-niche. Your target market comprising a specific age group and gender will be YOU. The frustrations will be YOURS.

Why? Because you can currently relate to these issues personally. Or you might target a younger age group because you can remember vividly the struggles, needs and values of that stage of your life.

Your Micro-Niche should consist of people who you would enjoy connecting with and people who would equally enjoy connecting with you.

If you are not a vegetarian don't make it part of your niche just because you think it makes business sense. You will either get found out as a hypocritical meat-eater or you will end up hating your business because it's not a good fit.

Choose a micro-niche that you identify with personally, with genuine concern and interest.

Use a Sniper Rifle, Not A Shotgun

Intuitively, people believe that taking a general, encompassing approach is more effective but evidence shows it is not. When you try to catch everyone in your net you catch no one. The 'cast your net wide' or more graphically the heavy artillery shotgun approach to business is well and truly dead.

A broad approach is especially ineffective when you are starting out. You need to become a laser-sharp marksman focusing on a very specific micro-niche.

Here are 10 general, boring answers I've heard to the question *"What do you do?"*:

1. I'm a consultant who helps businesses grow.
2. I work in the health and wellness industry.
3. I have an IT services business that keeps your systems running smoothly.
4. I have a marketing agency. We can pretty much help you with anything you need.
5. I design websites, blogs and e-commerce platforms.
6. I'm a personal fitness instructor and I help people to lose weight or tone up.
7. I'm a Chartered Accountant but don't hold that against me!
8. I import furniture and other goods.
9. My wife and I are starting up a business doing training programs for corporates.
10. We shoot video for businesses. We can do anything.

All 10 of those answers will get a polite response from the person who asked you what you do. None of them will get you any real business. None of them will open up the floodgates of opportunity.

Those answers are boring and general. They don't really exclude anyone and they create no density or gravity to what you do.

Here's how I would improve the previous 10 answers to question *"What do you do?"* that would ensure a better response:

1. I consult with small cleaning businesses. I only work with companies that have less than 20 people and I only work with the Director or Marketing Manager. After building and selling my own commercial cleaning company I'm confident of my specialty which is helping these types of business create contracted revenue then groom for a sale.

2. I work with women in South West London aged 30 - 49 who have very slow metabolisms and put on weight easily. I construct a specific diet plan that speeds up my clients resting metabolic rate and allows them to worry less about food.

3. I run a boutique IT company that recommends and installs special phone systems in call centers that have more than 40 sales people. We allow the sales managers to silently track and listen in on sales calls.

4. I have a marketing agency that specialises in selling products to 15 to 18 year olds in Bristol. We have the ability to test or survey up to 10,000 teens in this age bracket before launching any new product to a wider market. Since 1995 our entire focus has been getting into the minds of 15 to18 year olds and now we know exactly what they want and how they want it.

5. I design blogs. Just blogs. All I do is help people to have a stunningly good-looking blog that gets read and

that people keep coming back to again and again.

6. I'm a fitness instructor who works with skinny office-workers, men aged 28 - 35 who want to bulk up and get big shoulders, arms and chests in under five months.

7. I'm a chartered accountant who works exclusively for consultants and contractors who are one-man-bands. I make sure their shoebox full of receipts actually gets filed and they pay as little tax as legally possible.

8. I import rare, exotic, exclusive, one-of-a-kind boardroom tables and chairs. We ensure the boardroom table fits with the unique brand of the businesses we work with.

9. My wife and I used to work for the largest sport sponsorship firm in Italy. We developed relationships with all the big Italian brands and we now have our own company here in central London that helps UK sporting event organisers access the sport sponsorship budgets of Italian brands.

10. We shoot orientation and training videos that are designed to be shown to new members of staff in their first week. We capture stories about the values of your business and the specific things they need to know in order to represent your organisation correctly from minute one.

These 10 examples are loosely based on real-life successful businesses I know of. They aren't even 7 out of 10 responses, yet they have generated a lot of business and opportunity in the real world and they are engaging.

Building Strong Foundations In Your Pitch

Once people are engaged by what you do, next they will be interested to know some more. This is where you must know your stuff so well that it comes from your heart more so than your mind.

You know you have it when you can talk passionately about your topic for three minutes or three hours. Getting to this point requires you to start with some structure.

Let's take a look at some key things you need to know about your pitch.

Your Idea Centers Around A Problem

There is no value in coming up with an idea that doesn't solve a problem in a better way. There's two types of problems that are valuable to solve:

- Something people or businesses are already doing/ buying which you can provide better, cheaper, more conveniently, with more emotional benefit;

AND/OR

- An unsolved problem people or businesses have or will have soon (as a consequence of technological, economic, political or social change) which you can solve.

You Idea Is Based In Reality

For your pitch to have real power and value for others, they need to know that your idea is based in reality. Ideas based in reality are almost always born from one of these three insights:

1. **A Customer Insight.** One day you were shopping for something and you just couldn't find what you were after. The service you received was terrible, you discovered something shocking or you just knew that it could be done much better in some way. So you set out on a mission to right all the wrongs that you saw as a customer.

2. **A New Technology Insight.** You've spotted a way that technology can be created in a way that solves a real problem or offers a brand new benefit to people. You see that there's some new opportunity to combine your niche with a new technology and make life easier.

3. **An Industry Insight.** You know your niche so well that you've been able to figure out how things should be done better, faster, cheaper, more consistently or with more fun.

Your Idea Is Aligned To You

When people hear you talk about your pitch it must tell them "why" you are doing this. A good idea will not hold your attention long enough if it doesn't line up with your strongly held beliefs, so it's important to articulate why this idea is perfect ... for you.

What strongly held beliefs do you have that make this more than just a good idea; it's an idea you are *"born to do"*?

For me, *I believe that in the entire human history there has never been a better time for people to discover their passion and turn it into a profitable business that also makes difference.*

This is a strongly held belief I have and I know businesses that line up to this belief keep me focused on them long enough for them to succeed.

Whenever I have tried to go after a good idea that didn't really line up with my beliefs, I tired of it quickly and it fizzled into an expensive learning experience.

Quick Exercise ...

What strongly held belief do you have that makes you perfect for your big idea? "I believe that .....

....

....

....

....

....

....

Your Idea Delivers Clear Benefits

Next you must answer *"what"* are the benefits you bring to others. You need three core benefits that others will experience as a result of aligning themselves to you.

For example, when I designed the "Key Person Of Influence" products and services I knew I wanted to promise three main things:

1. You get to earn more money with less struggle.
2. You get more recognition and industry fame.
3. You get to attract more of the right opportunities for you.

No matter what I do with the Key Person of Influence products or services I always ensure that these three things are being delivered for people.

Quick Exercise ...

What three things (valuable promises) do you want to give to others? "With me, I promise you will get ...

....

....

....

....

....

....

Your Idea Can Be Delivered

Once we know *"why"* you want to do something and *"what"* it will do for people, the big question most people want to know next is *"how"* will you deliver it.

Will this be a consumable product? Will it be a service? Will it come as a subscription? Is it a training program? Is it a web site? Will it be a retail store? How you get your value to others may be in many forms and it may grow over time.

Richard Branson has a big why ... *"to shake up old industries and give customers a more delightful experience"*. Virgin delivers three main promises: to give customers a better deal; to make its service fun, and; to champion the needs of regular people. How they deliver it is through trains, planes, credit cards, phones, festivals and about 150 other businesses.

Quick Exercise ...

How do you get these three valuable promises over to others? "If people want what I have to offer they can ...

....

....

....

....

....

....

When you know the foundations of your pitch life gets easy. With strong foundations in place you can easily give a talk, write a brochure, create a new product, author a book, record a video or do a deal.

The most important next step is using these foundations in a nice logical order to share your ideas with others in a way that allow them to get enrolled in your vision.

I have found that there are "Six P's" for pitching that will give you a steady, flowing conversation whether it's a quick conversation or a 13 hour flight from Singapore to London.

Position...

It's clear to your audience who you are and why you are worth listening to. You might state this yourself, you might be introduced by a respected friend, you might arrive in your Private Jet (as any billionaire will tell you, the real value of a Private Jet isn't the leg room). In a simple example you might position yourself by saying something like *"I'm Mohammed, I'm a fitness instructor and I've worked with people who use gyms for the last 22 years."*

Problem...

You have seen a real problem and you are calling attention to it. Your pitch might continue by saying, *"After working with so many people I noticed how very skinny guys consistently struggle to bulk up and put on muscle."*

Projection...

You know that this problem impacts greater areas of life than one might first think. You project forward into the future and stipulate what implications can arise if this problem isn't dealt with. You could say *"When a guy is working out every other day and he still isn't getting results his confidence suffers and it can be demotivating in all areas of life."*

Proposal...

Then you suggest that you have a way of solving this problem. You might say, *"I have a diet and work-out plan designed especially for Skinny Guys aged 25-35 who want to bulk up with muscle."*

Proof...

You want to back up your claim with some proof that it's a good idea, if you haven't got proof you can have a highly respected person who vouches for what you are saying. Maybe you say, *"I've worked with 35 men now and all of them added over 3kg of muscle in three months which is enough to show a visible transformation. I have had this independently verified by one of the UK's top sports scientists."*

Project...

Finally you share what you are currently working on to take the idea forward. You might finish by saying, *"Now, I'm looking for a joint venture partner who can market this method to gym's and personal trainers."*

It might seem a little too structured at first however with practice you will develop so much clarity in your own mind that you will be able to talk about your idea naturally and still hit these bases in the right order.

Public Speaking and Media Appearances

By far one of the fastest and most powerful ways to become a Key Person of Influence quickly is to speak to groups either at live events of through the media.

As a speaker you are instantly transformed into an authority on you topic and you speed up the time it takes to get your message out.

One of the essential things all KPI's must do is get comfortable giving their pitch to a group. If the thought of public speaking or being featured in the media scares you, it's time to enroll into a speaking course or work with a professional to ensure you can get your message across to a group as powerfully as you can in a one-to-one meeting.

Organise your pitch into a talk and ready yourself for the day you get invited to take the stage or appear in the media. It will also help you in Steps 3 and 4 of the KPI Formula when you go to create a product (Such as a CD or DVD) and an online presence (Like videos on YouTube).

"That won't work!"

A big fear people have when sharing their idea is getting the response *"that won't work"*.

One of my mentors in the UK, Mike Harris, has raised hundreds of millions of pounds sterling for his projects. (You can get his book Find Your Lightbulb on Amazon). He tells me all the time that one of the best responses you can get when you tell someone your idea is "That won't work!"

Rather than getting offended, Mike see this negative reaction as an excellent opportunity to find out what people think is currently blocking the way forward.

If someone says to you, *"That won't work"* ask them why they think it won't. Be patient, ask lots of questions and write down the answers. It's these valuable insights that will draw you to discover the most important elements of you pitch that you need to get across.

If someone says that it won't work because *"You won't find good staff who can deliver the specialised service"* then your next pitch will become even more powerful when you say, *"A big reason this hasn't been done before is because it's almost impossible to find the staff needed to deliver the service. We have been able to overcome that issue and here's how..."*.

Some of your best insights will come from your critics and success will be that much sweeter when you prove them wrong.

Perfect Pitch Powers Performance

Your Perfect Pitch is your foundation. From here we will turn your pitch into a book, a product, an online presence and get others involved through JV's and partnerships.

Without a 'Perfect Pitch' you should be cautious about completing the next steps in this book (by all means read them, just be sure that getting the pitch right happens first).

A poor pitch will yield a boring book, impossible-to-sell products, traffic-less websites and fruitless partnerships.

You want to be sure that what you have to say is valuable, you are excited by it and others can get excited too (or easily see it's not for them). You want to be sure you are happy about your micro-niche and the part you want to play in it.

If you're happy with what you have created then get ready for the next step in the 5 Step KPI Formula.

You are about to see how to get an express pass to the inner circle of your industry.

Bonus

For a special audio download of my mentor, Mike Harris, talking about Perfect Pitch and creating an iconic brand, visit:

www.keypersonofinfluence.com/perfectpitchbonus

KPI STEP 2:
Write, Publish & Distribute a Book

When you have a 'Perfect Pitch' a big question people will have (whether they say it out loud or not) is:

"Why should I believe you can do what you say?"

A lot of people come up with big ideas every day, however very few people can attract the right team and get a project to complete.

People need to know that you are:

a. Able to come up with credible insights for your business idea, and

b. Trust your ability to get things done.

A published book communicates some important and necessary messages about you.

It says that you have put enough thought into this idea to have a book on it. People can read your ideas and get to know your story and your take on things.

It also says that you must be either an expert or have access to experts. We assume that in order to write a book, you must have some expertise in this field or you must have been able to interview people with an expertise.

Additionally people can see that you can complete a project. Very few people have ever published a book and for most people it's impressive to know that you have completed this project.

Finally a published author is often well connected in their field. In writing a book you will be able to pick up the phone and talk to all sorts of new contacts for input into your book. If you have written a book then chances are you are able to attract the right people around you.

Imagine when you meet people and say, "I am the author of a book on my industry, and in writing the book I discovered a potential business opportunity that I am currently working on".

Now people are interested. This wasn't just anybody who came up with an idea; it was an author of a book. And if this person has what it takes to write a book they could clearly start a business in that field too.

You might be a bit worried about writing a book. Maybe you don't have enough content to fill a book, maybe your ideas aren't special enough. Maybe your ideas aren't special at all.

These are all concerns that many (now) published authors had before sitting down and writing their book.

A friend of mine is a writing coach. She has helped over 300 people to plan, write, publish and promote their books.

She's absolutely convinced me that there is a book in everyone if they follow a process and commit to its completion.

Why Produce This Book?

The first thing you should do is construct some real reasons you want to write a book.

Is it because you want the money? Do you want 'best-selling author' on your CV? Do you want to be featured in the media? Do you want to create something that will outlast you?

These are all good reasons to write a book and I am sure you will have some other reasons that will excite and motivate you too.

It's important that you get clear on the benefits you want to achieve from your book before you begin the process.

When the writing gets tough you need to be able to imagine yourself getting the things you want out of life as a result of your published book.

Different Types Of Books

Fortunately, there are a few different types of books you could write and each one has unique benefits.

Here are five types of books you could write:

1. Your Take On Things

This is a book you can write based on your story and your background. It's full of your ideas and insights. This book is a 'Your Take On Things' book. This book might have a title like:

"Energy Foods
- A guide to eating foods that make you come alive"

"Making a Home
- How to decorate your house to feel like a home"

"Speaking Like A Pro
- How to give a powerful 60 minute talk"

The advantage is that it gives you plenty of room to demonstrate your ideas and your unique take on things. You are the star of this kind of book because it's you sharing your insights.

The disadvantage is that you will need to have at least 60 A4 Pages or about 25,000 words to fill a small book. It can be quite daunting to get 8,000 words into writing and realise you are only a third of the way through.

2. Book Of Interviews

This is a book where you find existing KPIs and feature their stories or their ideas in a book. This kind of book might be called

"Advice From 25 of the UK's Most Effective Fitness Trainers"

"Secrets of the Best Interior Designers in London"

"Success Stories from Real Life Wedding Planners"

"100 Up-and-Coming Short Film Makers in New York"

The advantage of this type of book is that you get to go and meet these existing KPIs. Very few people can resist the idea of being featured in a book and will happily sit for hours answering your questions for the book. You may even be able to record the interview and make them into a product (more on that later).

The disadvantage is that you don't get to be the star of the show. Your KPI status will improve as a person who must be well connected but not as a thought leader yourself.

3. Book of Tips

This is a book full of quick tips and rapid fire ideas. It might be called something like:

"101 Ways To Market Your Hair Salon"

"99 Things Every Real Estate Agent Should Do To Get The Best Price"

"125 Questions To Ask Before You Buy a Vintage Car"

The advantage is that this type of book is easy to write. You can list off 12 main categories of interest then come up with 12 tips for each category. Now you have 144 tips, it will take you less than two months to write the book if you complete three tips per day.

The disadvantage is that these books can seem a bit scattered. They seem not to delve deep into a topic and they appear to be the "easy option" to writing a book.

4. Picture Book

For some industries you might be better off showing lots of pictures rather than words. Clearly if you are a photographer or a fashion designer people would be much more interested in pictures rather than words. Your book might be called:

"100 Years of Political Fashion - Pictures of the fashion worn by politicians of the last 100 years"

"Landscapes of Asia - A photo guide of the most beautiful places in Asia"

"Great Old Cars - Photos of vintage cars and the people who collect them"

The advantage is that people love looking through picture books and they tend to sit on coffee tables rather than book shelves. It's also a very easy book to create in short runs through a number of online picture book publishers.

The disadvantage is that this book probably needs to be printed in high quality colour, using high resolution photos and it can get costly to produce.

5. A Creative Piece

This could be a parable with a message or a fictional story. The advantages are you get full license to make up as much as you like and it's very much an expression of your creativity. The downside is few people are skilled enough as a writer to get this genre right and it has little value to you as a KPI if the message doesn't come across. My opinion is to leave this genre to the pro's unless you feel a strong calling to write this style of book. Some good examples are *Wink and Grow Rich* by Roger Hamilton, *Who Moved My Cheese* by Dr Spencer Johnson and *The Alchemist* by Paulo Coelho.

Once you have decided on the type of book you will produce it is very important to consider the following:

The message of the book

My writing coach says that a great book answers a significant question that the reader is trying desperately to answer.

Your readers may be asking themselves:

"What do successful managers do that I don't?"

"How do people become wealthy when they are starting from scratch?"

"Why do some people eat what they like and stay skinny while I put on weight if I look at a pack of crisps."

The reader's core question forms the underlying theme of your book and each chapter, interview or section is giving another key piece of information that answers this question for the curious reader.

Planning the book

Before you even lay your fingers on the keyboard to start writing your book you must plan your book.

When you plan your book, you put the key question on a large piece paper and brainstorm all of the connected questions people in your micro niche might ask. Explore the content you need to share with them to fully answer their questions.

When you've done that you need to arrange your ideas into chapters of a book and then brainstorm your chapters in the same way.

If you spend one to two hours really mapping out each chapter, writing the book is a breeze.

The more you plan out your book, the easier it is to write creatively and the better your book will be.

Planning your book is also an excellent exercise for your mind. Mark Twain famously said, *"The time to begin writing an article is when you have finished it to your satisfaction. By that time you begin to clearly and logically perceive what it is you really want to say."* His sentiment is that through careful planning you can formulate your vague thoughts into clear, articulate and tangible ideas that will spread.

Choosing the title of your book

Whatever type of book you produce, one of the most important decision is the title. Many more people will hear that you are the author of'The Tittle You Chose' than those who actually read the book.

You might like to call your book something vague that only makes perfect sense once read to the end. However your book will lose impact with a cryptic title. If you introduce yourself as"I am the Author of The Race"people can't tell what you are a KPI in. If you introduce yourself as 'the author of The Race Towards A Greener Scotland' people instantly understand that you must be a KPI in Scotland for green issues.

Don't wait until you have the perfect title before you create your book. Quite often several titles will hit you while you're writing.

When you're ready, make a list of at least five potential titles and run them past a few people to see which elicits the best response.

Go to a networking function and tell people you're writing a book called"________". Watch their response and see if they pull out their phone to put you in touch with some relevant people. If so, you're onto a winner.

My belief is that you should choose a title that reinforces that you are a Key Person of Influence. It should be 'brand enhancing' and you should feel proud to tell people that you are the author.

A Writing Coach

I recommend getting a writing coach. Earlier I mentioned my friend who has helped more than 300 people to write, publish and promote their books. She is a genius at making sure your book is outstanding.

There is a lot to learn about writing a book and getting it to sell. If you can afford to work with an expert like her, you should do it. She can offer you a professional perspective and coach you to produce your best work.

So many people say they are 'working on a book' but few actually get it published.

Don't get caught in the trap of getting half way through several book ideas. The book has no power until it's finished and a writing coach can help you to get your book completed and on Amazon in under twelve months rather than 36 months (Imagine what an extra 30 months of being a KPI is worth).

A writing coach can also help you to produce your very best work.

Publishing Your Book

In the past, getting a publishing deal was an essential part of becoming an author. Only publishing houses had the money and the power to print a large quantity of books and then get them distributed.

Today there are boutique printers and small publishers who will print your book in very small runs on demand. There's no reason you can't print 50 copies of your book to see how well it sells.

In the past, it was pointless writing a book because you simply couldn't get in distributed without a publishing deal in place.

Today you can have your book distributed world wide through Amazon. You can set up an account online as an author in a matter of minutes and within a week your book can be shipping all over the world from Amazon's warehouses.

More importantly, when people do a Google search on you they can see that you are an author.

Promoting Your Book

There are many ways to promote your book if you want to focus on marketing however it is not vital

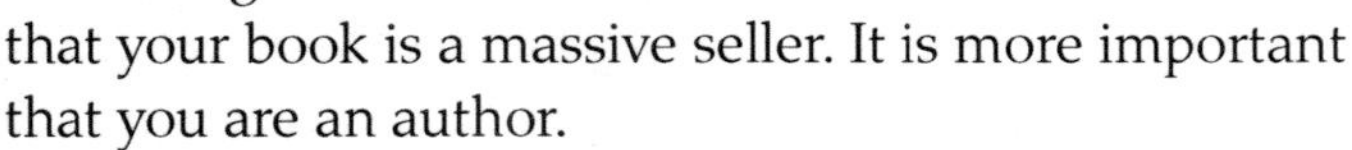

that your book is a massive seller. It is more important that you are an author.

Each year less than a dozen books sell over a million copies. Most books don't sell more than 500 copies a year.

That's fine! If you use your book correctly it won't need to sell millions. The purpose of your book is to promote you, not the other way around.

The mere fact that you are an author and that people can see you on Amazon gives you more kudos and opportunities.

You will find that it is easier to get invited to speak, to get publicity in the media and to get face to face with key contacts once you are an author.

In later chapters I will share some Social Media strategies to promote your book if you want to. But it is completely acceptable if your book only sells a few dozen copies each year.

Remember, it is not authors who get great opportunities, it is KPIs. Your goal is to become the Key Person of Influence in your industry in under twelve months, not to spend all your energy trying to sell books.

Books Make Credibility Products Make Cash

Your book will be a brilliant tool for getting clear on your thinking, for getting recognised as credible and for connecting to the right people however as a product the margins are small and the shipping is expensive.

Action step

I have a video of my favorite writing coach giving a talk at an event. Go to this link to have a look:

www.keypersonofinfluence.com/authority

Are you ready for the next step?

In the next chapter you will see that a great product can be high value, low cost and open up all sorts of opportunities.

If you are ready to turn your skill-set into an asset

... read on.

HALF WAY POINT

How are you going with *"the hidden theme"*?

You are half way through this book, have you got it yet?

Here's a hint from Victor Frankl's book, Man's Search for Meaning (1946)...

> ***"Everyone has his own specific vocation or mission in life; everyone must carry out a concrete assignment that demands fulfillment. Therein he cannot be replaced, nor can his life be repeated, thus, everyone's task is unique as his specific opportunity."***

Keep looking, keep connecting the dots and if needed, re-read this book a few times until you get it.

KPI STEP 3:
You Need A Product

Two hundred years ago the wealthiest people owned tracts of land and sprawling farms. One hundred years ago the wealthiest people owned massive factories and bustling production lines. Today the wealthiest people simply have big ideas that spread like wildfire.

We now live in the Global Ideas Economy. The successful people who make money and win the accolades are the clever communicators who can make an idea take off.

One of my favorite authors, Seth Godin says that *"Finding new ways, more clever ways to interrupt people doesn't work. It's the person who knows how to create an idea that spreads that wins today"*.

Products Make Money and Spread Ideas

One of the best ways you can really share your ideas with a vast number of people in an effective way is to create an information product. This might be a CD, a DVD, a USB Drive or a Download. Such products are not an interruption either, they are means of communication that consumers chose to participate in.

If packaged correctly such products have a high perceived value even though the cost to produce them is small.
A CD might only cost £1.50 to produce but have a value of £49 depending on the content. A 12 DVD workshop with a workbook and some phone support can sell for as

much as £5,000 (These figures are based on real cases of colleagues I know personally!)

As well as having excellent margins, a product builds relationships. If someone takes an hour to listen to your audio CD they feel rapport with you, they bond with you and really start to understand what makes you unique.

You start becoming the person they MUST do business with rather than a person they COULD do business with. You shift from Functional to Vital.

Products Expand Your Opportunities

Imagine that you get invited to be a guest speaker at a seminar for 30 minutes. (Random invitations to speak are quite common for a respected author.)

You agree on the condition that you can promote your CD set for £50. At the end of the talk, you say, *"If you like what you just heard and you want to know a little more, I have a special offer for my CD Set"*.

If 20 people out of the group decide to buy your CD set, you just got paid £1000 for a 30 minute speaking spot. Go You!

This may also lead to a lot more business too. Each person who listens to the CD set is more likely to want to do business with you in the future as well.

Rather than it being logged as an expense to talk at a local function, your product allows you to become a highly paid speaker and continue the relationship with all the people who enjoyed your talk.

Products Don't Sleep

If you are your product, being paid for your time, this presents a big problem. You only want to work for about a third of the day, right? And you can only be in one place at any given time. There will always be a limitation on what you can earn if your earning capacity is based on your personal appearance.

Products are expansive and liberating because you can sell them online 24 hours a day, seven days a week and they can be delivered all over the world. This one fact alone is a key reason you must develop a product on your journey as a KPI.

Will Your Product Be Valuable?

Some people say we are drowning in information and no one would buy an information product anymore. That is not the case, if your perfect pitch was done right.

If you want to sell an information kit on some general subject like *'How to be a good parent'* I admit, it probably won't sell. However if you have honed your micro-niche and created a product like *'How to be an amazing single parent, while still working your high pressure job in London'*, you will find that parents with this same challenge will beat down your door for your advice.

It is easy to get this stuff wrong. People spend a lot of time and money producing lame duck products that just lack value. Don't even begin to make products until you know you have a well-developed micro-niche.

If you create a product that helps solve a very real and specific challenge that people have, it will sell.

Every Business Has Ideas Behind It

You may be wondering how this applies to an un-glamorous business like cleaning, photocopying, stationary or logistics. Should these more traditional businesses create an information product for their clients too? Absolutely YES.

Regardless of your business, it is the ideas behind your business that make it special and prevent you from having to constantly compete on price.

In order for ANY business to stand out from the crowd it need to have some great underpinning ideas. People want to know what sets you apart or at the very least what is 'your take on things', before they get excited about you and feel happy to spend a little more.

Imagine a dry cleaner that gave it's customers a CD explaining *"Why we treat every garment like it's a valuable asset"*. Regardless of whether you listened to it or not, you would be blown away that they put so much thought in.

Imagine a men's fashion outlet that had a DVD featuring an image consultant sharing ideas on *"How To Look Slimmer, Richer and More Powerful For Less Than £500"*.

Instantly, you start thinking about spending £500 with that store.

Imagine a restaurant that had a CD from the chef talking about his commitment to sustainable, ethical farming. Just seeing a CD called *"Why I choose to pay more for my ingredients so that you can feel good about your meal"* would make you feel good about paying a little more at the end of your night.

No matter what industry you are in, you need to share the ideas that make you special. Tell people why you prepare your products the same way your grandmother showed you.

Explain to them what's so special about the way you deliver your service. Give them a peek behind the curtain at some of the things you take for granted but your customers never knew.

Make A Product For Your Competitors!

There's also a lot of information that you take for granted that your 'competitors' or counterparts (people like you who operate in different markets) would be interested in.

Maybe your restaurant business is great at saving money on wasted food because you have a clever system you came up with. That product could earn you more profit than your restaurant does!

An industry specific product can be worth a lot of money and make you one of the most respected people in your field, opening you up to Joint Ventures and Partnerships.

Creating Your Product

There are several types of products that can be useful for your business.

Let's take a look at three great types of products you could easily create:

A Free Audio CD/DVD/Download. Everyone should have a free product. Everyone! And that does mean you. The person who will dominate your industry in the next ten years will be the one who is able to give more away for free than anyone else. The fastest growing companies in the 2000s were all companies that gave away incredible value for free - Google, Facebook, Twitter, LinkedIn.

The best thing you can give away for free is an information product that educates people why they should do business with you. I want you to make it a goal to have a CD, DVD or Download that you can give away for free so that when people listen to it they are thinking "This person really knows their stuff" or "This person is super connected" and they want to do business with you.

There's nothing you can create more cheaply that has more value than an information product that shares your experience and insights with your potential clients.

An Information Kit. An information kit can be something you sell for serious money. I know a couple who built a successful eBay business turning over about £250,000.

They then created an information kit on how they set up their eBay business, sourced products and marketed them. That information kit generates over £750,000!

Consider what you know that you could turn into an instructional guide. Is there something that people already ask you to teach them? If it comes up, again and again, it could be an indication to you that there are people all over the world who want to know these answers too.

A Set of Interviews. Sometimes you don't even need to be brilliant in order to create a brilliant product. If you are able to secure a telephone interview with some of the top people in your industry, record it and produce a CD set of interviews, then you've got something of value and you become a KPI by association.

Here's A Secret ... Share Your Secrets!

Here's a big secret. Don't keep secrets. Share your best ideas with everyone.

Consider that the most famous chefs share their recipes every week. The more they share the more their value goes through the roof. You don't hear people saying, *"Now I have Jamie Oliver's recipe, I will never visit any of his restaurants again"*.

The more people have the more they want, so share your ideas freely. You will also make room in your mind to have even better ideas.

The more people have the more they want, so share your ideas freely. You will also make room in your mind to have even better ideas.

Speaking With Confidence

Surprisingly some people are more afraid of talking to a plastic voice recorder than they are talking to a real life person. It's worth investing into some voice coaching or public speaking training if you are self-conscious about recording yourself on audio or video.

Speaking with confidence is about being in the right state and practicing some good techniques. A great trainer can help with both. If you plan on making a good quality product its an investment worth making.

Getting Your Ideas Into The World

We live in a digital age where it's actually cheaper to think globally than locally. The technology is now available for you to transfer your ideas, your pitch and your products to people anywhere in the world for free.

If you don't know how to create a powerful presence online then you will miss out on sharing your products with people who want them in parts of the world you never knew existed.

In the next chapter we make you "web-famous" so that when someone Googles you they can see straight away you are a KPI and they can begin to get excited by your ideas.

If you are ready to open up to opportunities all over the planet, turn to the next chapter and read on (after you complete the exercises of course).

Action step

Check out this cool video ...
www.keypersonofinfluence.com/product

Exercises ...

1. If you had a free CD to give away what would be some amazing value you could record on on it?
2. If you had a 12 DVD workshop that people would pay £1000 for what would it teach people?
3. What are the valuable secrets that you could share on a CD/DVD or Download?

Get to it ... Make time to record your product.

Notes ...

....

....

....

....

....

....

....

....

KPI STEP 4:
You Need to Google well

You need to get 'Web-Famous"'. When people google you, they want to see some videos, some blogs, a few photos, some community groups you are part of. They want to be able to make friends with you and download your ideas and cross reference them with their own ideas.

Nothing is more disappointing than meeting someone who seems interesting, but nothing comes up about them on Google.

You Have A Rich 'Media Mogul' Uncle
Imagine that one day you get a letter from your rich uncle who just happens to be a Billionaire Media Mogul. He's devastated that you have been estranged for all these years and he wants to make it up to you.

He says that all you need to do is video record yourself and he will distribute it worldwide for you for free on his network!

He says that if you record some audio, he will have it available on air all over the world.

He says that if you write an article, he will publish it and make it available in all corners of the globe.

What would you do? Would you write back and say,

"Sorry, I'm really a bit busy right now. I'm not good with technology and I've never done it before. I'd rather not promote myself to a global audience ... but thanks all the same."

If you are reading this kind of book, I'm sure you would drop everything to take up this great opportunity.

Well the reality is that someone IS making these offers to you. There are free opportunities to get your videos, audio, articles, images, and ideas out to the world right now through social media.

Even better still, Social Media shares your ideas with people who are genuinely interested in them rather than trying to force them onto the mass market.

Why Water The Concrete?

When I launched my first business at age 21, I did what most people in my industry did to generate leads; I took out an ad in the paper.

I still remember the nervous feeling as I read out my credit card numbers to the ad. rep. who had sold me the $7,000 (Aussie dollars) quarter page display ad.

I asked the question: *"What percentage of people who buy this newspaper fit into my demographic."* I was targeting men aged 45-60 who had white collar jobs and were fed up with their current service provider.

She answered, *"I think about 10 per cent of our readers would fit into that category"*.

Ironically, I looked out the window as she was talking to me and saw the neighbor had set up their sprinkling system in such a way that 50 per cent of the water was landing on the concrete driveway.

Why would anyone waste their resources? Why would you spray 50 per cent of the water onto infertile ground? Why would I spend my marketing money on ads that aren't right for 90 percent of the audience.

When I took out that first display ad, $700 was spent talking to my market and $6,300 was just wasted. On top of that, my money had to pay for paper, journalists, delivery boys, news agents, managers, editors, ink, print presses and truck drivers. The cost of producing a real paper and getting it to people is huge.

Social Media allows you to talk directly to your market and everyone else can go look elsewhere. It's also digital so there are much lower costs of production and distribution.

In short, Social Media allows you to have a long conversation with people who care about what you have to say for almost no cost whatsoever. You would be mad not to use these powerful tools to promote yourself as a KPI.

Six Objectives For Your Social Media Strategy

I have six clear business objectives that I meet with my Social Media campaigns:

1. To generate leads and enquiries

Sites like Wordpress, Ecademy, Twitter, Facebook and Slideshare are absolute gold-mines for generating leads.

Earlier I talked about the need to give away as much as possible for free. Social Media allows you to give enormous value to the world for free and it comes back to you in the form of leads. Additionally, a lot of referrals these days happen through social media.

How many times have you heard someone say, *"Google Fred Smith Limousine Hire Manchester"* or *"Look in my Facebook friends for Mary Brown"*. You want to make sure that you get found when someone is recommending you!

2. To convert leads and enquiries into sales

Imagine you go to a web site for an accountant. When you get there, you find videos to watch, audio podcasts to download, ebooks, slides and blogs to read.

Is that going to make you far more likely to do business with them? It sure does. Without a doubt, the more time a potential client spends with you the more likely they will buy.

3. To increase the amount people spend

When people know more, they buy more. After years in sales and business I have discovered that a buyer will spend about seven hours deliberating over a substantial purchase. Whether it is a big TV, a training course, a car, a three-month coaching program or an overseas holiday, consumers take about seven hours. If that's the case, you want to occupy as much of that seven hours as possible. You want them to be listening to your podcast, watching your videos, following your twitter feed and reading your blogs.

4. To increase the frequency of purchasing

If you genuinely believe in what you're offering, you want regular sales. In this busy world people can simply forget about you. But not if they read your blogs, see your Facebook updates, follow your Twitter feed and subscribe to your YouTube channel. Keeping people up-to-date, results in more purchases per client, per year.

5. To find ways to reduce wasted costs

Sure enough, you can use social media to reduce your printing and customer care costs, but the big one is the saving you make compared to untargeted advertising. Without Social Media you will probably be advertising in a local paper with less than 10 per cent of readers even remotely interested in what you offer.

The beauty of social media is that it's free, or very low cost AND it's targeted precisely to people who are interested in what you have to say.

6. To improve the overall brand of the business

There's nothing wrong with having a great brand for your small business. A consistent message that is all over the internet is a valuable thing when it comes time to raise investment or sell your business. It's also great for your team to see as well as suppliers and Joint Venture Partners.

Becoming "Google-able"

When you Google search a KPI it's clear who they are, what they look like (photos and videos), what they have to say and how to get in touch with them.

It's not difficult to pass the Google test if you embrace Social Media because Google rates information on these main websites highly.

Some of the must-use sites you can use to make yourself Web Famous are (bear in mind that this list will probably date quickly):

- **YouTube.com** : The largest video broadcasting web site on the internet.
- **Slideshare.net** : The Number One place to share your Microsoft Powerpoint and Apple Keynote slide presentations.
- **Facebook.com** : The largest online social network where you can have your profile and your business page.
- **LinkedIn.com** : The biggest online directory of professionals.
- **Ecademy.com** : One of the most supportive small

business social networks on the web and a great place to blog.

- **Wordpress.com** : An excellent place to blog (a blog is like a journal).
- **Twitter** : The micro-blogging site that is also an excellent place to listen to your customers and the industry leaders you admire.

If you have a presence on these web sites and you take some time each month to keep your profiles up to date, Google will love you. It will begin to send people your way when they search for your name or keywords it finds in your profiles.

Your followers, friends and fans will love you too because they quickly get to know you through your videos, photos, groups and articles.

It's important to remember however, that your success online can only be as good as your perfect pitch. If you're message isn't strong you'll be wasting your time or worse, you might even be damaging your brand.

This also brings us back to the value of learning to speak and write well as a KPI. When it comes to content that you are putting online, be sure that it represents you well because you never know who's looking.

Social Media is like a microphone that amplifies you out to every corner of the world. Most people are too busy playing with the technology and go too far"off message".

I give talks all over the world on Social Media Strategy - If you want to have a look at some of my slide presentations visit *www.slideshare.net/triumphant*

The Magic Of Social Media

The final scene of the movie *The Last Samurai* shows Tom Cruise running into battle with his Samurai comrades dressed in their proud warrior kimonos with their glimmering swords drawn ... only to be met by fumbling 22 year old soldier wielding a brand new gatling gun.

As a shower of bullets rained down on the confused samurai, their final thoughts must have been that the beauty and tradition of their craft simply couldn't stand a chance against this new, powerful, magical technology.

This must be the feeling in corporate offices across the world who have taken too long to acknowledge that Social Media is not some little fad. It's the very reason their best staff have left, their customers aren't buying and their profits seem to be dropping.

Their customers are being met with more engaging competition and their huge profits are being dispersed to budding entrepreneurs all over the world.

Social Media has changed the way we work, play and even relax. More than ever it's the way people chose to engage with businesses, organisations and individuals.

Those who are using social media effectively can't help but feel like they had just been given magical, super powers. We now have the magical powers to read the minds of any great leader, celebrity or friend through Twitter.

We have the super power to stay connected with every person we've ever met through Facebook.

We can broadcast ideas, memories and opportunities to the world on video, audio, images or text through YouTube, Slideshare, Flickr or iTunes.

We can see and hear what's going on all over the planet, live as it unfolds through UStream and Online Media.

We can answer every question we can dream up in as much detail as we care to know. Google, Wikipedia, Slideshare and Yahoo Answers ensure you never have an unsolved mystery in your mind except of course the deep philosophical question *"What will I do with all of this information?"*

Strangely enough it is all free, meaning that this immense power is no longer in the hands of the few.
It now belongs to the many.

A cool hippie-chick recently said to me that she wished she would be around to see a"shift in global consciousness on the planet".

Unfortunately for her, she isn't spending enough time online to witness it. Magical shifts are happening right under the noses of anyone who has embraced Social Media. For a KPI, these shifts can mean magical shifts in your bank account too.

The best is yet to come

Whatever you do, don't worry that you have missed the boat on this new technology. It's just getting started.

The first five years of social media was simply platform building and people were just using it for the fun of it. We will not see the full effects unfold for many years into the future.

I remember my grandmother telling me about the excitement she felt about a new rail line that connected her up to a big city when she was a teenager.

Realistically though, it wasn't the train or the tracks that was so exciting. The new rail line meant she was able to access a whole new world of possibility faster than ever before. New people, new ideas, new resources and new inspiration.

She wasn't the only one who saw the possibilities. After rail lines, highways, phones and air travel connected people in the first 50 years of the 1900s a global boom in creativity occurred.

By giving designers, engineers, entrepreneurs, investors and entertainers access to new markets the world saw new music, entertainment, medicine, technology and products unfold to an unprecedented degree.

It is the same story throughout history. Before every boom in creativity comes a new way to connect – coaches, cars, phones, trains, planes. When humans can connect fast, we can create fast.

Today, the world is buzzing with excitement as we see Facebook, Twitter, YouTube and Skype turn the big wide world into a standard feature in the living room.

However, let's not forget that the last ten years have seen technology focused on new ways to connect and share information at greater speed. This is the "Rail Line"… The real excitement comes from the fact that there is a whole new world of possibility on its way!

We are about to see the perfect environment for another boom in creativity. Designers, entertainers, entrepreneurs and everyone else can collaborate at a whole new level and faster than ever.

An inventor in India can talk to an investor in London who can pay for manufacturers in China to deliver a product into Sydney. All of which could be done easily and quickly, without big businesses slowing down the process.

There is no shortage of people talking about how bad things might be in the future however keep in mind that there is no shortage of new ways to make exciting progress as well.

I predict a creative boom in art, entertainment, medicine, architecture, fashion and technology that we can barely comprehend right now. In every one of these fields there will be hundreds of micro-niches and in each little niche there will be Key People of Influence.

The real trick now is for KPIs to connect with the right people and do the best deals possible so that everyone's value is leveraged at a higher level.

When you are ready to see how to make all your work pay off, turn the page for the final step in the KPI Formula.

Bonuses
Check out this great video ....
www.keypersonofinfluence.com/webfamous

Conect with me:
www.twitter.com/DanielPriestley
www.linkedin.com/in/DanielPriestley
www.facebook.com/dpriestley
www.slideshare.net/triumphant
www.vimeo.com/DanielPriestley

KPI STEP 5:

You Need to Do Joint Ventures & Partnerships

What I am about to share with you is the secret that separates the KPIs who make BIG money and the KPIs who are well known and liked but still don't make the sort of money they are worth.

The key is Joint Ventures (JV's) and Partnerships. This is where you get to multiply time and achieve extraordinary results rapidly.

Consider that someone in your city has already built a relationship with thousands of people who could be your clients. That list is on someone's hard drive right now.

Someone already has some free products that they would happily add into your product range just for the exposure.

Someone already has a great brand and is looking for some great products to endorse.

Just as you have worked hard in the last five years to create your pieces of the puzzle, someone else has worked just as hard and is holding onto the missing piece that you need. When the two of you connect up, the money can flow at an alarming rate.

When I first arrived into London with just a suitcase and a credit card, I literally knew no one. It was my first trip above the equator!

I had no network at all, but I knew that I had an exciting product that had a track record in Australia, New Zealand and Singapore. It was a product especially designed for entrepreneurs, so the first thing I did was to start searching for the existing KPIs in London who were focused on serving entrepreneurs.

Through a friend of a friend, the first people I met with were Thomas Power and Glenn Watkins of Ecademy.com (an excellent social network that supports entrepreneurs). They loved the product I was launching and said they were happy to help.

Thomas suggested that I host a dinner party for about 40 KPIs of entrepreneurship in London and invite them to get involved.

The dinner party was a great success. It cost about £1650 and it ended up generating several great JV's and partnerships. In our first week over 800 people attended our events and we made over £100,000 in sales.

Rather than running expensive advertising campaigns, we built an affiliate system that automates our JV deals. In the following three years over 1000 people joined up as affiliates and helped us to generate over 50,000 bookings to events and millions of pounds in revenue.

JV's Come In Many Shapes and Sizes

There are several types of JV's and Partnerships that I recommend you look into:

1. An Affiliate System

This is a system that tracks where every sale came from and pays a commission to the person who helped generate that sale.

It's not a new concept (accountants and lawyers have been paying 'finders fees' for years), but with modern technology you can really ramp it up.

Imagine you launch a website selling t-shirts for £25. The front of the site is a normal looking store however there's also a back end for affiliates.

When an affiliate logs into the site, they are given a special link. They are told that anyone who arrives at the site through this link, and buys a t-shirt will be logged as their affiliate sale. They might make 20 per cent of all the sales they make.

As an affiliate they are free to use email, Twitter, Facebook, blogs or videos to promote your site.

The more people who click the link and buy a t-shirt, the more money they make. And so do you.

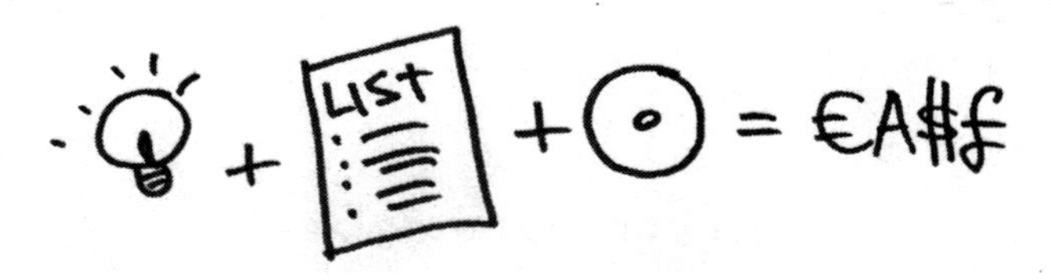

As I said, we built a big events business using this model. If you want to look at our custom built Affiliate System visit www.triumphantevents.co.uk/affiliates (create an account and have a look around the back end of the system. You might even want to earn some money while you are there by promoting our upcoming events!)

2. Mail-Swap

This is when two companies with similar sized databases each mail their contacts about the other person's offer.

Sometimes the lists aren't exactly the same size so you need to agree on how you will get around this. One company might add some money into the deal or mail their list several times to make up the difference.

You will quickly discover that some of the people who never respond to your offers are suddenly interested in the new product you offer as part of the mail swap.

I have had people tell me that they have a list that doesn't respond to anything, when they mail this so called 'dead-list' with our offer we soon find out that there's about

£10,000+ worth of business in it.

3. Product Teaming

This is where you team up with another person or a group to create a more valuable new product.

Imagine a personal trainer teams up with an image consultant and a photographer to create a 'Complete Makeover' package for £990. It's a great way for all three businesses to work together and help the client to get the best result possible.

Always approach this with the question: *"What is my client REALLY trying to accomplish when they work with me and who could I team up with to get an even better outcome?"*

In the above example, the client isn't looking to lift heavy plates of metal, spend money on cloths or sit around smiling at a cameraman. They want to tone-up, look fashionable and get some great photos while they are looking at their best.

By thinking about how you can help your client 'get something done' you will be able to identify who can help you to help your client.

4. Packaging Up

This is very similar to Product Teaming except you are looking to add someone else's existing products into your own existing products. Imagine you are a restaurant and you are next to a cinema. You could do a 'Movie-Meal Deal' and capture more customers and extra revenue.

5. Free-Bundle Group
Everyone likes free stuff. Even better they love bundles of free stuff. Why not team up with several businesses to put together an irresistible free 'basket of goodies'.

Let's imagine that you have a Free Meditation CD you give to potential clients, the Yoga Studio down the road gives away a Free First Lesson and a chiropractor friend gives away a Free Spine Assessment. If you do a JV, each of you now has a very nice free offer you can use to attract new business and promote each others businesses.

How easy would it be to generate new leads if you created a Free-Bundle worth over £300?

...Yeah, exactly!

Getting Started with JVs and Partnerships

All the time I hear people say, *"I just had a good idea but how do I actually make it happen?"*.

Firstly, you should never ask, *'HOW do I make it happen?'* You should ask, *'WHO do I need to talk to?'*

Whenever you have an idea, no matter how crazy, make at least three calls to see if it's doable.

Making three calls can yield you some amazing results.

My first real business was running underage dance parties with my best friend when we were just 18 years old.

Originally we were planning on hiring an industrial shed but we soon discovered it would be a nightmare to run a party there and almost impossible to make money.

On the off chance, I called the number one nightclub in town and told them we wanted to run a dance party for teens on the school holiday. I asked if they would meet with us to discuss a potential Joint Venture.

They agreed to see us and we put forward a deal that made sure they would cover their costs with no risk and get lots of positive PR. They signed a deal on the spot.

Next we went to the local radio station and asked them to partner with us too. They agreed that in exchange for sponsorship rights, they would give us free radio advertising.

Six weeks later we ran the biggest teen dance party in the area that year and walked away with more cash than we could carry!

I learned a very valuable lesson. Whenever I have an idea now I always pick up the phone and make three calls just to see what might happen. I am always surprised at how much can happen in just three calls.

When I started Triumphant Events at age 21, I had the audacity of calling some of the best people in the industry to see if I could work with them to promote our events. They all said yes and the business turned over a $1million in its first year of trade!

When I launch this book, I will be calling up people and asking them to join my 'Amazon Best Seller' team. This team will have the sole purpose of launching this book and making it an 'Amazon Best Seller'; in exchange I will be sharing some of my best strategies with the team on product launches.

It sounds like a good idea, so I will make three calls and if you see this book advertised as a 'Best Seller' you will know that it worked!

Exercises ...

What three calls can you make right now?

1. Three people who already have a list?
2. Three businesses that give away free stuff for your bundle?
3. Three people who you can team up with and make a product?

What three calls could you make (regardless of how scary) that could really get your ideas off the ground?

Go for it!

Notes ...

....

....

....

....

....

....

....

Go Networking For JVs and Partnerships ... Not Clients

One of the key differences between KPIs and everyone else is that KPIs don't go out looking for clients, they go looking for partnerships and JV's.

Going out to a networking event looking for a client is like trying to get to China on foot. If you want to go to China, you don't want to go one step at a time, you want to figure out who already flies there in a jet.

KPIs only go networking to find leverage. They are looking for people who have a big database of clients, a channel of distribution, a great brand, an awesome product or some other key aspect of value or leverage.

I often get frustrated when people come up to me at a networking function and try to get me to become a client. I almost always like it when someone is thinking about a mutually beneficial JV.

To step things up as a KPI, forget looking for clients and start looking for relationships that can really make things happen for both parties.

- *Do they have a list of potential clients?*
- *Are they interested in co-producing a product?*
- *Have they got a product that would be attractive to your contact list?*
- *Is there a beneficial contact you can put them in touch with?*

These are all powerful questions that yield better results than *"Can I make a sale right here and now?"*

A KPI is not interested in chasing sales. A KPI knows that their goal is to attract the right types of opportunities and the right opportunities for a KPI will always be win/win.

The money is in great partnerships and joint ventures. Whenever you want to take your income up to a higher level, go looking for a higher level partnership or joint venture.

Meeting a Potential JV or Partner

It can be nerve racking sitting down with someone who has the power to double your quarterly sales with a single email. You want to make sure you get a few things right so that the deal goes ahead and the relationship is long lasting.

Set The Scene

I always meet people in either a private members club or a nice restaurant. I don't meet people in my office or theirs because the spirit of a JV should be about meeting on common ground to create a win/win/win (you win, I win, the customer wins) deal. It creates the wrong starting point if one person has to make the trip to the other persons office. I also like meeting in nice locations because a JV or Partnership should be about creating wealth and abundance for everyone involved.

Bring A Gift

When I meet with a potential JV Partner I like to bring a thoughtful gift to show that I am thinking of their needs. It might be a copy of a book I would recommend for them or even something simple like a magazine article clipping I think they might be interested in. It's not to demonstrate that I am spending a lot of money on them, it's to demonstrate that I am already thinking of their needs.

Make Friends First

A deal will not normally happen if you don't like each other even if the deal is perfect in every other way. Conversely if you do like each other you will find it easy to make a deal work.

I normally talk about anything other than business until I am sure I like the person and they like me. I don't do this as a trick or to win favour, I genuinely want to do business with people I like and share common ground with.

Do Business Last

When you know you have rapport and it seems entirely appropriate to bring up business it should only take 15-20 minutes to make a deal work at a top line level. Much longer than that and it might not be a good deal to be doing.

Always go into a meeting with a fair deal in mind and know in advance what you are flexible on and where you can't budge.

Pick Up The BIll

I am personally a fan of genuinely offering to pick up the bill. For me it shows that I valued the meeting with them. Of course if they insist on splitting the bill I am ok with it, because it shows we are both thinking 50-50 even on small things.

Follow Through

After a meeting, allow 10-15 minutes to follow through on anything you mentioned you would do. Sometime in the course of conversation you might say that you will email through a web site address, a name of a book or connect two people on email.

Very few people actually follow through on these off-hand remarks, but it gets noticed when you do follow through and it sends a powerful message that what you say and what you do are the same thing.

Now it's time to do it

Why do so many people fail to achieve anywhere close to their full potential?

The ideas in this book are simple and they get consistently favourable results for people who do the work. So what will hold you back? Why do many people fail to move forward on good ideas when they know they should?

Hitting these 5 bases

What I have shared with you may seem simple. I've given you just five things to focus on, however never underestimate the power of simplicity.

In-built into these five outcomes for becoming a KPI you will find that there is Clarity, Credibility, Visibility, Scalability and Profitability.

Over the next 12 months I can guarantee you that my inbox will be full of people emailing me their success story.

I already know what they will say. Their email will tell me that they did the work, pushed through their limiting beliefs, made the time and did all five of the steps in order (it's very important that you do the steps in order). They will then tell me that "like magic" opportunities started to come their way, more money began to flow and they started to have more fun.

They will tell me that they experienced three big benefits after doing the work set out in this book:

1. They earn more money with less stress and struggle
As a KPI, opportunities come and find you, rather than you having to go chasing them every day.

2. They enjoy greater status and recognition in their industry
As a KPI you become someone who is "industry famous" and this means that you get to have more fun, meet interesting people and do more meaningful work.

3. They attract more opportunities that are right for them
As a KPI, you often pick up the phone and find there's a perfect opportunity that has just come your way. It's also easy to get opportunities to gather momentum. You can call in favors as a KPI, you have more cards to play and the projects you get involved in flourish as a result (which is why people call you in the first place).

I desperately want *you* to be in that group. Yes, you (the one with the eyeballs fixed on these words)! I want your story in my inbox telling me that you have done these 5 simple things, made yourself an opportunity magnet, earning more money, having more fun and creating more success.

Sadly, there's a good chance you won't be. People can get addicted to the struggle and let complexity get in the way of simplicity; the unimportant stuff replaces the most important stuff or worse the desire for immediate quick wins creeps in.

Over the last 10 years I have studied peoples buying habits like a hawk. As a marketing person I am insatiably interested in human behavior and watching people trying to make decision for their life.

In the next few chapters I will share with you some of the things I have noticed when watching highly successful people make decisions versus people who are perpetually frozen between the headlights of life.

The next chapters will offer some ideas on how you can overcome the obstacles and become the Key Person of Influence in your chosen field faster and without as many struggles.

Action step

For a great little video on identifying who you could be doing joint ventures with, watch the video here ...

www.keypersonofinfluence.com/partnerships

Part 3

MAKING IT HAPPEN

Unfortunately our brains are mostly geared to look for quick easy wins. Your mind will play all sorts of tricks on you to stop you from making it big. We need to know what we're up against and how to overcome the obstacles that get in the way of becoming a Key Person of Influence.

You Can't Do It Alone

By now I hope you see the power of Partnering or Joint Venturing with others. It saves you years and a lot of money to find the right person to JV with.

Well it doesn't end there. The most powerful way to save time, money and mistakes is to learn from others who have walked the path before you.

I am always surprised when someone tries to do something on their own. I'm convinced that some people want to create an 'original mistake'.

In this age it's possible to find someone who has done what you want to achieve already and learn from them. It's called standing on the shoulders of giants.

Creating a book or a product could potentially be difficult, time consuming and expensive. Why would you risk your time, energy and money without the right support.

When left alone, most people will not complete any of the KPI Key Outcomes to their full potential.

It's almost a cliche that people are 'working on a book' and can let countless hours of great content slip through their fingers.

You may have already done this. Consider every talk you have given could have been a podcast, every meeting could be an interview for a CD set or a book.

The truth is that we will never achieve our full potential on our own. That's why every great sports person has a coach, that's why the president has advisors and why great actors have a director to bring out their best.

It's encouraging having someone to push you and bring out your best work. Right now, I am writing to a deadline and I have someone keeping me accountable. I also have people who I respect and admire who will read the draft so I am pushing myself to perform.

Unfortunately most people who attempt to hit these targets on their own make costly mistakes. They procrastinate and waste time and too often they create an inferior product that fails to create the desired outcome. It may even damage their brand rather than build it.

It is disappointing to see someone on video who has nothing unique to say. They talk in general terms and create no gravity to their ideas. They were given the gift of having a captive audience then blew it with amateurism.

The other important point to remember is whatever you put online is there for life. Getting it wrong can leave you with content that keeps coming back to haunt you.

Without the right guidance people over-commit to needless expenses (like high cost printing, design, filming,etc). They spend their time and money in the wrong area. Nothing really links back to their business model and it all looks a little sad.

Why would they do this when the best experts are available to help? You don't need to make the mistakes that someone else has already made. There are people who have achieved the goals you have set for yourself and they can help you get there faster and better.

For every project I am involved in, I surround myself with the KPIs in that field. If I'm writing, I make sure that the expert who is helping me has written successful books themselves and helped others do the same.

If I am working on my Perfect Pitch, I want to work on it with a mentor whose Pitches have built dream teams and made millions in profit.

Give yourself the gift of leveraging the success of others and make sure you get yourself some support and guidance from people with results while you are on your journey to become the Key Person of Influence in your industry.

Find yourself an accountability buddy or better yet, a coach to push and guide you. Paying for their support will also ensure you follow through and get a return on your investment.

When I first heard about ILR. I was shocked at how many great opportunities I had lost over the years because of this phenomenon.

Cars, business growth, houses, travel, friends, mentors... the list goes on!

It became an obsession to make sure that I dealt with it and got rid of it as best I could.

ILR stands for the 'Illusion of Limited Resources'.

Why would I claim that it is an illusion that resources are limited?

Professor Paul Zane Pilzer who was an economic advisor to several US administrations (but not the last two) says that a resource is only defined by our ability to use it. Effectively there are no resources without resourcefulness.

The only reason oil is a resource, is because we are resourceful enough to use it for so many things. Before we understood it, it was nothing more than black sludge.

Chances are, you are already standing on an 'oil well' of opportunities that are just waiting for you to become resourceful enough to see them.

If you don't believe me, try to imagine if tomorrow morning Richard Branson would swap lives with you for a year. He would get your house, your car, your friends, your family, your challenges and even your bank account.

Imagine he would even have to take on your name and appearance. In 12 months when you swap back, do you think there would be some noticeable changes?

Of course there would! He would spot opportunities that you had overlooked. He would pick up the phone and have conversations that you had not been having. He would start to introduce himself more powerfully than you currently do.

What about poor Richard when he has to go back to his life in 12 months. If you hadn't been as resourceful as him, he might find that his island had been repossessed, his planes grounded, his managers had all quit and his space ship was missing!

We all want Sir Richard's resources but very few people are willing to get even a little bit more resourceful than they currently are. After reading this book, I sincerely hope you are willing to stretch and do what it takes to become the Key Person of Influence in your industry.

No matter what you need in your business or your life, getting it will be a function of your resourcefulness rather than whether the resources are available. Of course they are available.

The three biggest factors that determine your resourcefulness are:

1. The Questions You Ask
2. The People You Know
3. Your willingness to stretch into the unknown

Let's take a look at these three factors in the next chapters.

The Questions You Ask ... Determine The Answers You Get

If ever I hear myself complaining about not having access to enough resources I know I need to look at the questions I'm asking myself.

If I've been complaining, chances are I've been asking *unresourceful questions* like:

"How come I can't find the time?"

"Why is this so hard?"

"Why can't there just be an easier way?"

"Why do I have to do this, why can't someone else do it?"

I know straight away that I need to ask a better question and immediately, if I do ask a better question I will get a better answer.

Here's some *better questions*:

"Who would absolutely love the chance to work on this project and would be able to do an amazing job?"

"What value can I add to this, that very few people could?"

"How do I make this even better?"

"Who has already achieved this result in the past?"

"Who woke up this morning who already has access to the resources I want?"

Requests Versus Opportunities

In tough times many people focus on the resources that they want and they aren't shy about telling everyone. You hear some people say things like...

"I need more sales coming in. Can you help me make more sales?"

"I need my team to get motivated. Can you get me a motivated team?"

"I want more qualified leads. Can someone get me some better leads please?"

"I want my suppliers to give me a better deal. Can I get a better deal from suppliers?"

All of these are just requests. Unless you are a child, asking your parents for something small, the language of requests does not work very often.

You need to learn the language of opportunities. This is where you win, by helping someone else win. When you want something, you express it in a way that works for the person you want assistance from. Here's some examples:

I need more sales coming in. Would you like to follow up on some red-hot leads and get 10 per cent of the money you bring in?

I need my team to get motivated. If I could see an improvement in performance I would happily share some of the upside with you. What kind of conditions would make that deal a win for you?

I want more qualified leads. If we can get more targeted leads we will save a lot of wasted time and money, I would be happy to share some of those savings with you. Who do you think we should stop targeting with our campaigns?
I want a better deal on supplies. If I ordered in bulk would you be able to offer me better terms?

Great business people speak in the language of opportunity ALL the time. In the next week, see if you can eradicate all requests from your language and adopt a policy that you only offer opportunities.

You'll be astonished at how many people will get excited to work with you when there's an opportunity on the table as opposed to a request.

It's Not Just What You Know

Some people go to networking functions and collect business cards. They look at them proudly and think "Look at how big my network is." In truth though, they don't have a network, they have a pile of business cards.

A network is a group of people who share opportunities. You can pick up the phone to them, they happily take your call and they trust that you will have something valuable to say.

If you think of your network in those terms, how many people do you have in your directory that fit the criteria? How many people do you regularly share opportunities with?

If the number is low, you need to make this a major priority. You will NEVER sustainably increase your wealth without first increasing your network.

As a KPI this will be much easier than you think. People love being able to take a call from a person who knows what game they are playing, whose book they have read, whose CDs they have listened to and who they are connected to online.

With these things in place the quality of your network will develop at pace, but there's even more that can be done to ramp things up.

Firstly, get in the habit of spotting great opportunities for others. Quite often I will see something in a blog and email it to a friend. Quite often I will connect two people who I know can do business together. Quite often I will share an idea with someone if I think it would be beneficial.

I don't spot opportunities for friends because I am looking for an immediate reward. I do it because I believe that it strengthens my network.

Given time, a strong network leads to more wealth, more fun and more success.

New-Comers, Worker-Bees and KPI's

In every industry there are New-Comers, Worker-Bees, and KPI's.

The New-Comers are enthusiastic, excited and full of dreams. They believe that this new industry they are in will fulfill their dreams and take them places. New-Comers are normally willing to work hard with little pay in the short term on the belief that the rewards will come in later. Typically they have seen the results that a KPI has achieved and they want to recreate similar success for them self.

The Worker-Bees are the people in the industry who are doing the work but not getting anywhere. Some of the dreams have been knocked out of them. When they were New-Comers they thought that their industry was fresh, new, exciting and rewarding. Now it seems a bit stale and they are secretly resentful of the KPI's (for their effortless results) and the New-Comers (for their spark and enthusiasm). The Worker-Bees at some point may have enjoyed the work but are often disappointed that the results aren't coming in fast enough.

As we now know, the KPI's make it look easy. They always have lots of opportunity flowing around them and they achieve great results quickly. Their email inbox is full of people trying to get good opportunities to them. With a few phone calls they can make magic happen and get some of the spoils.

They also attract lots of New-Comers into their industry because they make success seem so easy.

The Merry-go-round of distraction

Here's what happens. Jaded Worker-Bees go buzzing about new industries and they spy a KPI. They get excited and decide to become a New-Comer to that industry. They feel the rush and the excitement that comes with a brand new project. They see how effortless success comes to the KPI in that industry. They think to themselves "I like what I do, but I don't get the rewards so if I can make easy money in this new field I can always go back to what I do and not worry about the money".

Like most New-Comers they get stuck in and do lots of work with little rewards. They expect that this work will pay off this time in the long run.

After a while, the New-Comer gets a bit tired and it feels like hard work. They have now met a lot of Worker-Bees in this new industry who say things like ...

> ***"It's hardwork in this industry, I've been at it for years and I still haven't seen the big rewards yet"***

The New-Comer becomes a Worker-Bee and begins looking around for the next big thing that will provide an easy win.

As this continues, they get further and further from pursuing their passion by constantly chasing the next easy win.

The answer to this conundrum is simple. You must focus on your passion and become a KPI in that field. As soon as you are a KPI you will not even notice opportunities in other industries because you will be swamped with great things to do in your own industry. And the rewards will come thick and fast.

There's no easy money, there's no quick wins for New-Comers or Worker-Bees - Not in property, not in shares, not on the internet, not in a franchise, not in a Network-Marketing business, not in a new technology - Easy wins go to KPI's. Period.

Resist the temptation to chase the new thing and keep taking steps closer to the inner circle of the industry you love. When you arrive as a KPI you will get your *"overnight success"*.

Stretching Into The Unknown

Most people believe that when the conditions are right they will act. This attitude does NOT work. Ever.

It's like saying that when all the lights turn green, I will leave my house and drive to work.

Not only do the conditions never become perfect for action. Most people won't act even if they were. Most people have become so used to not committing to things that when the time comes for them to commit they just don't do anything.

After witnessing thousands of human brains trying to make tough decisions I can now tell you that the people who are successful are the ones who commit to things that take them forward even when they aren't sure exactly how it will all come together.

I'm not saying to be reckless, I'm just saying that there's never a right time. You will *always* have challenges going on with either your time, your money or your focus. If something comes along that you know you should do, then do it and figure it out along the way.

Ready, Fire ... Aim!

Here's an example, if I decided that in order for me to write this book I would wait until I had a spare three to four weeks, it would have never happened. Instead I just started writing it.

I have written it on planes, in hotels, at all hours of the day and night.

I even wrote until 4 am one night, knowing that I would need to be up at 9:30am. It was difficult to get out of bed, sure, but after a shower I was fine and I made up the sleep later that afternoon.

A bigger example. When I was 24 I wanted to buy myself a BMW X5 with all the options. Despite knowing exactly what I wanted, I put off the decision for over a year. Then one day a friendly rival of mine bought himself a new BMW.

Well that was it, the next day I went down to the finance department and signed up for the lease and the car, not knowing exactly how long I could afford to make my payments.

After the lease was approved, it just became another thing I needed to find the money for each month, and sure enough I did it. There's no way I would have ever had that car if I had waited until I had 'spare' money lying around.

Richard Branson was in massive debt for the first 15 years of Virgin. Always getting letters from the bank asking him how he was going to pay for everything. Even in debt, he just kept buying more assets and signing more artists. Somehow he figured it all out, because he had to.

I wish the universe worked differently. I wish that you could plan to do things and then magically make time and money to then do them. It would feel a lot safer. But unfortunately I don't see that happening for anyone I know. The people I know over-commit themselves then figure it all out later.

Earlier, I said that ...

The more resourceful you are the more resources you will have. That's true, but here's the secret that few people share ...

Resourcefulness shows up AFTER you make a commitment

Prior to committing to something, half of your resourcefulness is working on overtime as to why 'this is NOT a good idea'. Without a commitment, humans use up too much brain energy on assessment of the idea, the timing and trying to predict an unpredictable future.

When you finally commit to an outcome, you free up gallons of energy to become more resourceful on following through.

Commit to a big goal (I mean literally sign yourself up to some sort of deadline or external commitment) and then start filling in the blanks.

Don't Work For The Clearing

Becoming a KPI doesn't happen for most people because they are waiting for the clearing. They think that 'one day' they will have the time, money and focus to get something done. So they keep working towards making a 'clearing'.

I ask them, "Why are you working so hard?" They reply, "So I can get some spare time and money and then I can go and do what I want."

No, no, no,no! Don't work for the clearing, work for the result.

Ask yourself what is it you actually want to do. Then go and do that.

There is no clearing. It never comes. You will be an elderly person in a home and finally you will realise that had you just gone for what you wanted you would have had it. A 'clearing' is not a goal. Bite off more than you can chew and then figure it out as you go.

If you were any good at creating a clearing in your life you would have had one by now. When was the last time you actually arrived at 'the perfect time and place with all the money you needed'. It's a fairytale.

If you suddenly realise that the most important thing you could be doing for your success is to write a book, then just begin it. If you know in your heart of hearts that you should be starting a business, then go start it.

I'm not saying you should be reckless, I'm just saying when something is important you should begin it now rather than waiting for all the lights to turn green.

If you are wrong about your idea, very rarely is the downside that catastrophic. In past civilisations, people who had bad ideas died. They were eaten by bears, burned at the stake, tortured to death or worse.

Today, the absolute worst thing that most people fear is the feeling of being a failure. People's worst nightmare is getting embarrassed because their idea didn't work out the way they thought it would! At worst they may lose some time and some start-up capital. Imagine trying to explain that to your ancestors!

> ***"Your ancestors would shake their heads in disgust. They faced wars, plagues and disasters to create a better world and you're not taking full advantage of all it has to offer"***

With the ideas in this book, the downside is NOTHING! I'm asking you to put some thought into your pitch, take some time to write, pluck up the confidence to record some interviews or a workshop and to use the free tools on the internet and go out to speak with a few people.

It will take some thought, it will take some time, you might need to spend a tiny amount of money and get some guidance along the way, but if you commit to doing these things you will jump to a whole new level.

You have virtually no downside in perfecting your pitch, writing your book, producing a product, using social media and talking to some people about a joint venture.

The upside, however, is *awesome*.

How To Get Back Over Seven Hours A Week!

Despite my efforts to encourage people to get started as a KPI, many people tell me that they are REALLY too busy.

I have a simple formula that will get back over seven hours a week (a working day) for most people.

Don't Watch The News.

Most television is a waste of time but the news is just a pitiful waste of time.

Absolutely nothing good will come from watching, or reading, the news. There is no way to justify sitting around watching the miserable events of the day. It is a huge waste of your time. It unconsciously jades your perception of the world, can make you depressed and doubt your ideas.

The average TV watcher wastes four hours on television per day. *FOUR HOURS!*

We are only awake for 16 hours a day and most people work for at least half of that. This means more than half of people's leisure time gets sucked into a vacuum … never to be seen again.

If you become aware of it, you'll notice that it's easy to use an hour per day watching or reading the news.

This is the time you need to become brilliant!

If something in the news relates to you, someone will tell you. If you still feel you must keep up to date with news use Google News to target the news you actually want to know about rather than passively waiting for the reporters to give you what's important to their networks ratings.

Instead of watching the news:

1. Go meet people for drinks or dinner
2. Exercise
3. Write your book, record your CD, and set up a YouTube Channel
4. Sit and think
5. Learn a new skill (Dancing, Kung-fu, Painting)
6. Volunteer your time at a charity
7. **Make the news!**

What to look forward to next

Remember why you are becoming a KPI. Keep focused on your big game and why you want to win.

> ***When you are a KPI you will find great opportunities come your way***

Fame, recognition, financial windfall, passive income, and other exciting opportunities are commonplace for KPIs. These things are nearly impossible for people who are not yet a Key Person of Influence in their industry.

Here are some tangible things to expect once you are a KPI ...

Media and PR - The Media is always looking for Expert Opinions, Feature Stories and Case Studies. Once you are a KPI start talking to the media and letting them know what you are up to in the world. Send journalists your book with your bio. When they have a relevant story they will think of you.

Speaking At Events - One speaking opportunity can generate seriously valuable opportunities if done correctly. Remember that speaking opportunities go to KPIs not great speakers. By the time you have hit the five main outcomes set out in this book, speaking opportunities will have already started to find you.

Directorships - Many companies are willing to pay sizable fees, or even equity, to have an established Key Person of Influence as a member of their board.

Your Own Networking Group - As a KPI, you can put together a monthly networking group. These groups can be a great source of income as well as a constant stream of opportunities. Chose a regular venue and start inviting people to come and join you. You will be amazed at how fast a monthly networking group can emerge.

Subscribers - As a KPI you can easily have and inner circle of subscribers who pay for premium content or contact with you. I know several KPIs who make over six figures (net) from their subscriber groups ... and their subscribers love them for it.

Random Surprises - KPI's get invited on fun holidays, the get sent free gifts, they get invites to be VIP guests at events and many other fun surprises show up unannounced.

Be sure to keep your eyes on the prize. The reason you are doing this is because all the best opportunities go to KPIs. As a KPI you will have more fun, make more money and enjoy more recognition.

If you don't become a KPI you will get stuck chasing revenue, spend too much time searching for (half decent) opportunities and forever feel undervalued.

The Power of Momentum and The Inertia

I hated physics at school. I remember thinking: what a completely pointless subject. What possible use will I have for this in the future?

Then I saw these two rules of the universe:

The Law Of Inertia - An object at rest will stay at rest, until acted upon by an outside force

These two universal laws have stuck with me since school and reminded me that when I feel the spark to do something, I should act on it straight away. Momentum is too precious to lose. It's a gift that comes far too scarcely.

If you feel compelled to act, then go for it. As you get going you will find that you gather pace and you get enormous amounts produced. Often I am happy to sit up until 3am in the morning working on something, just so I don't break the momentum.

Of course if you don't act you become governed by the law of inertia. You become an object at rest, destined to stay at rest until you get a big kick up the bum. Far too often the outside force that gets you to eventually act comes in the form of pain. You realise that you've not achieved any of your goals in two years. You lose a job. You lose a client. You lose a relationship.

Inertia weighs you down and it takes more and more effort to get moving. Momentum is the feeling of being in flow. It's a rush and it's the domain of creativity.

Why am I telling you this?

Because if you have read this far then deep down inside something is telling you that you are a KPI. You have a Perfect Pitch to share, you have an amazing book in you, you have a valuable product to produce and you have a worthy message to share with the world online. With those things in place, you will shine so brightly, that others will want to partner with you in sharing your value too.

It's time to stretch. It's time to invest your time and your money in doing these things. It won't be easy but it will be worth it.

You've read this book for a reason and that reason is to ACT. You're here to do it, not to learn about it. Enough with the learning, now is your time to become the Key Person of Influence in your Industry.

Action step

If you would like to explore the opportunity of working with a dedicated group of people that work with my mentors and myself on Becoming a KPI, read on ...

A few times a year we run a program called ***The KPI Accelerator Program***. It's the fastest way I know to get people producing their best work and rapidly moving towards being one of the most highly paid, highly valued people in their industry.

For more information on this opportunity, visit:

www.keypersonofinfluence.com/getstarted

KPI:
Case Studies

Lazo Freeman

When I first met Lazo Freeman he told me he was a Personal Trainer. I wasn't surprised, he certainly looks the part. After chatting for a while I discovered that he isn't just any Personal Trainer, he's actually a multi-award winning body builder. He's won major titles for Natural Body Building and he even won a competition to meet Cindy Crawford!

What did surprise me was that despite his awards, his hourly rate was only marginally higher than my Personal Trainer who had not won any awards. Lazo was charging about 30 per cent higher than the industry average.

Like many in his industry he thought that the key to his success was doing more courses, getting more qualifications and having a nice brochure. Lazo was working hard with his clients, getting great results but not seeing big financial rewards.

I started telling Lazo about my KPI Strategy and he instantly got it. He could see straight away that he hadn't differentiated himself from other Personal Trainers and he hadn't used his success to establish himself as a KPI yet.

The first thing we did was develop his *Perfect Pitch*. Today, rather than introducing himself as 'Personal Trainer', Lazo will tell you he does *'Radical 12 week body transformations with highly successful people who do amazing things in their work but very ordinary things naked!'* That line always gets a laugh, but more importantly, people want to see pictures of the 12 week transformations.

When Lazo pulls out his book and shows them some before and after shots of his clients, jaws hit the floor. In 12 weeks, Lazo can transform a skinny guy into a buff guy, a fatty to a muscle man. The transformations are extraordinary.

He then directs them to his DVD and invites people to make friends with him on his Facebook Profile.

By the time you see all of his photos, his YouTube videos and his testimonials you know that he is THE man for 'Radical 12 Week Transformations in London'.

Before you get too excited about getting him to work with you I had better inform you of what happened to his prices. Today Lazo charges £10,000 for a Radical 12 Week Transformation, and he has a waiting list! This makes him the highest paid "personal trainer" in London.

It wasn't the awards that made it happen. It wasn't the four years of getting outstanding results with his clients. It was becoming a KPI that caused a huge shift.

Lazo is now a KPI in his industry and is able to charge 500 per cent of what the normal person in his industry charges. He earns more than most doctors or lawyers and he has a lot more fun because he works in his passion.

Simon Dixon

Simon is driven, ambitious and genuinely likes to help people. He started out in the Banking and Finance World in a junior role and with careful planning as well as great work he climbed the ladder quickly.

By his early 20s, he was on the trading floor managing millions of pounds for his clients. In his late 20s, he had founded his own company and was working with the biggest companies in the industry.

Simon decided that he could provide an edge when it came to career development and founded a Recruitment Firm. Despite his success, after several years of running this business he still felt like it was a daily effort to keep things flowing. He had several sales people on the phones. He had an office and an admin team and he was personally going around London giving talks at Universities and Industry events. Simon described it as a constant struggle to win business.

When I first talked to Simon about becoming a KPI in his industry he immediately saw the value. There was no question in his mind that this could really make a difference. Little did he realise just how much.

Simon began by perfecting his pitch. He decided he only wanted to work with *'UK Students and Graduates who wanted a career in Banking and Finance in The City of London, and were committed to going from Student to CEO as fast as they could'*.

This meant that about 30 per cent of the people he had been trying to work with no longer fit with this new target.

He then wrote the book *From Student to CEO - 97 Ways To Influence Your Way To The Top In Banking and Finance*. From there he developed three DVD/Download programs that would sell for around £100 each.

Focusing on YouTube and his Blog, Simon generated thousands of new followers in Social Media and within a short space of time he was very google-able.

All of this positioned him perfectly for Join Ventures and Partnerships. Simon invested into an Affiliate System for his web site that would allow other people to promote his products and receive a commission. For the cost of one ad in the paper, he had the ability to generate new clients and only pay for results.

In the first two months over 350 people joined the affiliate program and started generating an average of over £800 per day in sales (with a 65 per cent margin). Completely automated. Every day new affiliates are joining up and using the system to make themselves and him more money.

Today Simon has no offices and third of the staff he used to have. He no longer needs sales people, instead he has an affiliate manager who handles the inbound enquiries.

Considering that his business is more profitable, more sustainable and more enjoyable, he's happy with his new status as a KPI.

As a KPI, Simon Dixon has been featured in the media and big companies are approaching him to partner with him. His business is no longer a struggle. It's fun again!

Penny Power

Penny Power will never need to worry about having enough opportunities. Today she has a personal network of over 10,000 people.

She has published an amazing book, *Know Me, Like Me, Follow Me.* She is web famous and is constantly approached by quality people with innovative ways she can reach more people.

Penny Power is pioneer in Social Networking. In the late 90s she started to get excited by the idea that through the power of online networks she could have a 'friend in every city'.

Sitting in a pizza shop in Farnham, UK, Penny decided she would get together with her friends and start a new web-based social network for small business people.

Her Perfect Pitch was fairly simple. She started out by inviting people to connect with like-minded business people in London to provide support, learning and networking online.

After that, Penny and her husband Thomas Power wrote the book, *A Friend In Every City*.

Today her business *Ecademy.com* has hundreds of thousands of members all over the world and is worth many millions.

She is also a KPI who is regularly asked to speak at events and appear in the media.

Sabirul Islam

At just 19 years old, Sabirul has sold over 50,000 copies of his book, *The World At Your Feet* and has created a brilliant board game called *Teen-trepreneur.*

He has spoken all over the world and has even been an advisor to government on youth issues.

Like many teens, Sabirul tried creating a small sideline business. Unlike many teens, at 14 he was designing web sites for big corporates like Merrill Lynch.

He was then accepted into a role as a junior trader, where he discovered quite quickly that his talents lay elsewhere.

The most unique thing about Sabirul is not that he did some interesting things as a teenager, but that he recognised the power in his own story.

He realised that other teens needed a role-model and that he could give them a unique take on things that few others could.

He wrote his book, created his game and spread himself all over the internet. After that, he was able to do several deals to distribute his products nationally.

This goes to show it's not time and it's not education that makes you a KPI. It's connecting the dots and seeing the value in your story, packaging it in the right way and doing the right deals.

For more KPI Case Studies of people that have used this 5 Step Sequence to become more highly valued and highly paid, visit:

www.keypersonofinfluence.com/successstories

Congratulations on reading this book

... and taking big steps towards being a truly connected, highly regarded KPI.

The book had some clear themes in it. You read about your *perfect pitch* to a micro-niche, *writing a book, making a product, becoming web famous* and *doing joint ventures and partnerships*.

All of these themes are important, however did you spot something else?

Did you notice a recurring theme that kept coming up for you? Did you connect the dots and see a hidden order that you weren't expecting.

When you do, you will discover that your future is clear, your past was perfect and you are present to the opportunities that are all around you.

After you spot the hidden theme:

> ***You will get a burst of energy; you may sit up all night writing, recording, producing and playing ...***

... and when morning comes you're still not tired. You'll feel good because everything clicked into place.

That's because everything was for a reason. Nothing was out of order, nothing was superfluous and nothing came along to hold you back. It was all there for the purpose of letting you discover what that theme is.

You may need to read this book again though. It's not the content that really matters, its the story behind the content. It's the chapters that are coming next that matter most.

Of course, the chapter that comes next may be at the beginning of this book as you keep looking, or they may be the chapters that you write for yourself. The important thing is that you find it and it's yours to share.

Daniel Priestley's next book is called '*The Entrepreneur Revolution - How to break free from the industrial revolution mind-set, quit working, follow a dream and make a fortune along the way.*'

Turn the page for a sneak peak ...

SNEAK PEAK:
The Entrepreneur Revolution

As a bonus for reading *'Becoming a KPI'*, here are the first few chapters:

Chapter 1:
The System you are in

I walk around and I see people living according to a system that makes very little sense to me.

I see people giving up the best part of their day, to push power to a vision that doesn't inspire them for a small amount of money that barely affords them an exciting life.

I see people who get stuck in mortgages that limit every decision they make. People who live in towns that they chose because they grew up there (but never looked anywhere else).

I see those who are friends with people who they don't respect or admire. They are friends just because they have always been friends.

I see people who are in religions and accept ideas that don't really make a lot of sense to them but they believe because everyone else does.

So many people are living in their past decisions. Or even worse, they are living in someone else's past decisions.

Over the last 150 years that hasn't been such a bad thing. The industrial revolution set the tone, working for a factory or a big corporation was the norm. As a worker you needed to be on site every day from 8:30am - 5:30pm, travel was something you had to squeeze into your annual leave, fun was something you can look forward to when you're too old for it.

The industrial revolution caused a massive shift in the way we live. Prior to this factory age, we were all entrepreneurs. We were butchers, bakers and candlestick makers. We knew the names of our customers, people knew our names (in fact they made our names from our little businesses - John Baker, Sally Tailor, etc).

Then along comes the machines. People who could afford to buy them multiplied their wealth and made ridiculous fortunes. Those who didn't have the means were swept up onto the factory floor to become faceless, nameless corporate slaves.

Once again the world is changing. The internet changes everything. It gives everyone new powers to create from anywhere in the world. It gives you a TV station for free, a radio station for free, a daily publication for free and a way of selling products and services for free. It takes all of this and distributes it for you globally.

It allows people to make money from tiny, silly little ideas. Radically, it allows people to make money from their passion. An idea that seems so foreign to so many.

What is to come is something that I call *'The Entrepreneur Revolution'*.

This is a new age where people are free to earn while they explore. Their personal breakthroughs, their journey of self discovery and their expression of creativity will replace the daily grind of the work place.

Now the 'factory' costs a few thousand dollars to set up. To be in business today requires you to have a laptop, a phone and an idea. This simple fact has given birth to a new breed of people who are part owner, part worker, part artist. The new breed of entrepreneurs have arrived.

Big companies will find it hard to compete with small ones. Small companies will reinvent themselves almost every year or two. People will matter again, causes will matter again and maybe we will see a world that works for a lot more people.

For me, this has been a discovery I have witnessed first hand.

I am an entrepreneur. In fact, I've never had a wage in my life. I founded my first company at 21 years old and have created several Multi-Million Dollar Businesses since.

Living out the Entrepreneur Revolution, it seems perfectly normal to travel when I want for as long as I want.

It's been normal to reinvent everything I do when I get inspired to do so.

It's a foreign idea to wake up on an alarm, to have a person who I think of as my 'boss' or to ask permission to get on a plane and go away for a week.

Through the miracle of Facebook, I have kept contact with my friends who haven't busted loose yet; the people who got good grades and then got good jobs.

I see that behind the great corporate titles are very boring jobs. Behind the annual holidays are people sitting at their desks most of the year counting down the days until the next break comes around.

It's a choice. Times have changed and we live in a unique time where if you want a steady job you can have one or if you want to make just as much money doing whatever you like, whenever you like, with whoever you like, you can do that too.

It's just as much effort to hold down a good job today as it is to be completely free as a bird. It's just a choice you make. Do you want to live according to the rules of the Industrial Revolution or the Entrepreneur Revolution?

This book is designed for people who want to live by a set of new rules. The Entrepreneur Revolution Rules.
I will take you on a journey. It's the journey I have been on and I will give you the lessons that I learned along the way.

Some of the lessons you might already agree with. Some may challenge you. Some may give you the key to the lock that opens the door to a whole new way of being.

If you're curious to know what it's like living in the Entrepreneur Revolution then turn the page and let's begin the journey.

The System You Can't See

It's time we had a very honest conversation about the crazy little system we have bought into and see what we can't do about gearing it up in our favour.

The system is made up of rules and ideas that were perfect for the Industrial Revolution but they are no longer right for people living in the Entrepreneur Revolution.

The system is insidious. It creeps up on you until it hums along in the background like an air conditioner or a computer fan. Most people can't see it, hear it, feel it and they certainly don't think about it.

Let's start with this simple idea...

"Work hard now
and you will get your rewards later."

This idea is in religion, in work, in government, in school and many other places you look.

The idea that you should sacrifice the moment for some far-off reward in the future.

It isn't the case. Right here, in this moment is all your power, all your joy, all your life-force. You have no power in the future or in the past, it's all here in this moment.

When you are present to your true feelings, you make better choices. When you project yourself into the future or the past you lose your power.

Agents of the Industrial Revolution controlled workers with the idea that in the future they would have great rewards for their labour if they suffered now. Some people are controlled by rewards they think they will receive after they are dead!

Reading this, you might start to feel annoyed. You might think that it is just the way it is and that I am mad for suggesting otherwise.

So, lets question it. *How long have you been putting things off for the future, and how is it working out for you?*

Surely if this idea worked, it would be really starting to show signs of producing results by now right?

Surely if you have been putting off life for 15 years there would be some pretty big rewards starting to stack up already ... surely if this idea works you could see the evidence starting to show?

For most people I speak to it hasn't started to show up... and if it has, the sacrifice wasn't worth it. They gave up the best part of their 20s and 30s only to spark a reckless mid-life crisis later in life.

For me the idea of passing up the most virile, energetic years of my life so I can take a few Euro-getaway-tours in my 60s is a complete non-starter. It's crazy!

Why play golf when you could have played anything. Why wait until you are too old to do the things you are waiting to do? Why cash in the nest egg when you could have been free as a bird in the first place?

One reason is fear. We are scared of living in the present because of what might happen in the future.

Ironically, from a place of centeredness here in the present we have our most authentic and powerful visions for the future.

The place to plan your future is in the present. The best place is on the beach, in a forest, or in a penthouse apartment ... whatever works for you.

If you are inspired you will create an inspired vision. If you are fearful you will create a vision based on mitigating your fear. It will be about scarcity and not abundance.

Another reason is that we are stuck with remnants of the Industrialised Worker Mentality. We think it's wrong to have fun all day, it's wasteful to sit and think, it's somehow bad to question authority.

You are stuck with old ideas that don't serve you and in

the next chapter we will explore some of them. If you are ready to flush out some old Industrial Worker ideas and replace them with dynamic Entrepreneurial ideas, then turn the page.

Chapter 2: Selfish Little Plebs

I want you to pick a number. This number is the amount of money you want to earn in the next 12 months. I am going to wave my magic wand and the number you write down will be yours. But don't be greedy.

It should be a number that satisfies all your wants and needs for the next 12 months.

Do it now.

Seriously. Go. Actually choose a number and write it down. £_____________________.

Write it down so you can participate in this exercise and really discover something. There is a right answer and you will probably get it wrong, but no one will know except you and me so you're safe.

How much did you choose? Was it twice your salary, three times, or did you lose your mind and write down something silly?

Surely you didn't write down millions ... tens of millions ... hundreds? A BILLION! ... oh please, Louise!

Tell me you wrote down a number that isn't selfish. Tell me you wrote down a number that isn't greedy!

If I find out you wrote down less than at least a Billion Dollars I will be disappointed and we have a lot of work to do on your greed and selfishness.

Greed? Selfishness? Why would I accuse you of that? After all, if you are like most people your number was probably modest and meek, you didn't ask for vast sums, you were *reasonable*.

Well here is the thing. I said, *'an amount that would satisfy all your wants and needs'*.

I am really hoping you have wants and needs that extend past you and your family. I hope you want to save rainforests, end hunger in far away countries, influence government policy, setup foundations, empower people, rescue animals, or something much bigger than yourself.

You just can't do that on £250,000 a year. You can't.

With £250,000 a year you can have a nice home, a nice car, a nice holiday, make a nice little donation and invest a nice little amount for your future and pay some nice taxes. That is it. You're not even able to do nice things for your extended family, your community, your local elderly, your local forest.

My answer is a little different.

I answer that question like this:

"I want the most amount of money that I can receive as a result of me being true to my authentic passions and inspirations".

If I am lucky enough to be like Bill Gates and my passion makes me a billionaire then I will rise to the challenges that Billions calls for. I may also do what he did and run one of the biggest charitable foundations on the planet too ... if that is my authentic passion.

If my passion makes only a small amount of money, but I am self-governing, free, and I am an inspiration to myself and others, then I will accept that too.

The important point is that it's not selfish to have a lot of spare time, or a lot of spare cash. It's selfish to indulge all of your time doing something that neither serves or inspires anyone and then make a boring amount of money that only barely compensates you for your greed.

The poor mind-set is the greedy mind-set

If you ask someone rich, *"What would you do for £1000?"* they would say, *"It's not about the money".*

If you ask a poor person, *"What will you do for £1000?"* They quickly demonstrate that they will give up the best part of their week for a vision that isn't theirs with people they barely care about and perform a role that they are only mildly excited by (if at all).

So who is the greedy one?

In my book it is the poor person who is greedy for money, addicted to money ... a slave to the filthy lucre.

It is the people with a rich mind-set who are mostly indifferent to the stuff. They are only interested in their vision, their passion, their companions, their adventure. You can't buy them.

So is this a state of money, or a state of mind?

Of course it is a state of mind. It is a choice you can make at any time. Of course you will need a vision, a passion, an adventure ... but that will come later in this book. For now I still have a few points I need to make.

What do you do for a living?

What do you currently do for a living? *Write it down ...*

... or at least say it out loud.

What did you write? Did you put down Sales Executive, Area Manager, Apprentice Plumber, Tree Surgeon, Town Planner, Activist or Architect?
Did you write down your job? Your occupation? Your source of income?

Why? Why did you write that? Why do most people think that what they do for income is what keeps them alive.

It's not! What keeps you alive is breathing!

If you ask me what I do for a living I will look at you strangely and say, *"I breathe"*.

At least in the short term. After that I guess I will need some water, some good food, a good night's rest and a sense of adventure when I wake will help I suppose too.

But I am really not scared of stopping breathing, or having access to water, food and shelter. I gave up my fear of that a long time ago. I have enough evidence to suggest that I am blessed to be in the small percentage of the world that will not be able to starve, or thirst, even if I really mess up. I have family, friends and welfare to fall back on until I get my wits about me ... if the worst should happen.

I also won't stop breathing for a long while. Even that is out of my hands. Whoever made us built in a funny little system that makes you pass out and start breathing again if you are stupid enough to hold your breath too long. But I digress.

The point is that we have built up a fear that what we do for income is keeping us alive. It isn't logical and it doesn't serve us.

It is an idea that the wealthy families don't have. If you asked Prince Charles what he did for a living he would be quite confused. When you explained that you were asking about how he sustained his place in the economy, he would tell you that *he is royalty and has an empire and he reigns over it.* You would think he is pompous, but he would go back to reigning and you would go back to trying to *make a living.*

Even self-made people are different. They all hate being asked that question. It is an icky question that is hard to answer if your well-off. Because the truth is, you do a lot of stuff, but none seems to directly cause you to be 'living'.

The truth is that wealthy people kind of 'reign' over their little empires more than 'work for a crust'.

If you asked me what I do for an income, my answer isn't simple. I have businesses, I am an international public speaker, I write, I have investments, but really that's not much of your business ... it's mine ... it is my little empire. And more to the point, it's not about the income! I do this stuff because it's fun, it's part of my adventure and I am inspired to do it. It just so happens that it produces income as well.

None of it is causing me to have a living. Most of it is part of my vision for my life.

So the big take-away from this little chapter is simple.

It's time to step out of the old paradigms of the industrialised working class and into the mind-set of the new rich. Forget "working for a living" and start building your empire.

This book is about to show you that never before in history has there been a better time to quit doing things that seem like "hard work" and start living your passion.

You are about to discover why "the harder you work the less you earn" and why you are ready and able to make your fortune from your passion.

If that sounds like an idea worth exploring, keep reading.

Chapter 3: Breaking out!

So rather than harping on about this mind-set stuff (because I do appreciate, the mere fact you're reading this book is evidence you're already on that path), I want to begin by giving you some real life challenges that will automatically start to break you out of this silly little system.

Let's begin by doing something crazy ...

"The Entrepreneur Revolution" is due out in 2011.

Daniel founded his first company in 2002 in Australia at the age of 21. Within 13 months the company was turning over approximately AU$1M. He has since launched over 9 businesses and products into new markets with most ventures achieving 6 figure sales in the first 3 months.

In 2006, Daniel moved from Australia to launch an office in London. Arriving with only a suitcase and a credit card, Daniel quickly set about building his connections in London. In the first 12 months of operation in the UK, Triumphant Events achieved more than £1M in sales and Daniel was considered as one of the Key People of Influence in his industry.

Daniel is in constant demand around the world and speaks to audiences throughout Asia, Australia, Europe and the United States.

He speaks from his personal experience of spending large sums of his own money on marketing and advertising, building sales teams, recruiting and retaining high performing teams.

Daniel has been able to build successful companies that continue to run even when he has been overseas for 6 months at a time.

Daniel is passionate about social entrepreneurship and is a business advisor and fund-raiser to several charities / not for profit organisations (or not for dividend as Daniel would say).

Lightning Source UK Ltd.
Milton Keynes UK
18 November 2010

163103UK00001B/2/P